DIVINE DISCUSSIONS
Higher Realms Speaking Directly To Us...

Phillip Elton Collins

The Angel News Network

Copyright © The Angel News Network

All rights reserved.

ISBN: 978-0692647790

Brief quotations embodied in critical articles and reviews allowed. Include the book's title, author's name, and the author's website (<u>PhillipEltonCollins.com</u>) as sources of further information. Contact the author via the above website to comment, for written permission regarding longer excerpts, or to otherwise use or reproduce this book.

Views expressed in this book are solely those of the author's perception at the time of writing. The author makes no warranties as to the accuracy, completeness, timeliness, or usefulness of this information. The author's intent is only to share information to help you in your quest for emotional and spiritual well-being. You are solely responsible if you use any of the information in this book for any purpose.

Because of the dynamic nature of the Internet, web addresses or links contained in this book may have changed since publication and may no longer be valid.

Cover images: PN M2-9:*T*win Jet Nebula. Credit: ESA/Hubble & NASA; Acknowledgement: Judy Schmidt. Comet Lovejoy. Credit: NASA/MSFC/MEO; Acknowledgement: Aaron Kingery.

Dear Humans Being Human,

It is your design and destiny that we of the higher realms connect with you at this time to assist your evolutionary ascension path. We assisted you in the creation of all your past golden ages and are here now to assist you again in the creation of your seventh and final golden age. Are you ready to receive our love and support? Have you had enough of the way things have been? Are you ready to activate your Divine Soul Plan by creating a world of equality, harmony and balance? All the teachings and tools you need are available to you right now to move into world service and free yourselves from yourselves by healing yourself.

Archangel Uriel, World Teacher with Adama, the Father of Humanity.

IN DEDICATION

This book is lovingly dedicated to the ensemble of higher realms with whom they and I mutually agreed, and chose to connect, through our Divine Soul Plans by bringing their teachings and tools into our reality in order to assist in humanity's advancement. My heart fills with gratitude for our connection and my humble service to you all: **Adama, Father Of Humanity; Akashic Records; Akhenaten/Moses; Archangels Gabriel, Michael, Raphael, and Uriel; Ascended Master Energies; Beings Of Cosmic Consciousness; Christ Consciousness Energy; Council Of Creation; Cosmic Keepers Of Creation; Cosmic Keepers Of The Akashic Records; Cosmic Mother; Council Of Archangelic Realms (CAR); Council Of The Galactic Federations; Galactic Federation Of Worlds; I AM Presence & Christ Consciousness Energies; Mother Earth; Saint Francis; and Your Creator.**

CONTENTS

Preface	xiii
In Gratitude	xv
Introduction	xvii
Alphabetical Listing Of Articles	1

A
A Conversation With Creation	2
A New Creation Story	4
A New Future, Five Fundamental Shifts	27
Accessing The Akashic Records	32
Adama's Message	39
Akhenaten/Moses And Me	43
Archangels Gabriel And Raphael	50
At Present	64

B — 66
Being A Channel Of Higher Realms	67
Being Co-Creator: From Child To Adult	76
Being Human	82

C — 83
Changing Your Comprehension Of Change	84
Coming Home To Your BEingness	88
Competition	94
Considering Karma	95
Council Of Creation	99
Creating Community With Creation	104

E — 110
Eight Sacred Principles Of Leadership	111
Ever Lasting Energy	113

H — 118
How To Quickly Change Your World	119
Human Cosmic Construct	120

I — 122
I AM: And So Are You!	123

K — 125
Knowing Rather Than Seeking	126

L — 127
Living Parallel Lives	128

M — 133
Me Or We, You Choose	134

N
	137
Nine Necessities: Agreeing To Be Human	138
No Failure	140

O
	141
Only Oneness Omits Isolation	142
Our Role In Healing	149

R
	155
Religions And Christ Consciousness	156
Rest In Peace 3-D	162
Resurrection: Christ Consciousness Energy (Transcending All Beliefs Into Cosmic Truth)	163

S
	166
Sacred Trilogy Of Teachings	167
Seven Sacred Flames: How To Use Them	168
Seven Sacred Flames: Daily Use	182
Sacred Shifts To Ascend	184
Seven Sacred Steps For Ascension	188
Seven Sacred Flames Chart	191
Seven Aspects Of Ascension	193
Saint Francis Energy	195
Separating From Separation Into Oneness	208
Some Ways To Love More	214
Spirituality And/Or Religion	215
Summer Solstice Letter	217

T
	219
Ten Tenets Of BEingness: Cosmic Commandments	220
The Cause And Cure For Terrorism	222
The Divine Gift Of Dreams	229
The Gift Of Commitment	233
The Meaning Of Life	234
The Returning Of Oneness	240
The Year Of The Starseed, 2016	245
Twelve Codes Of Consciousness	249

W
	251
What Does New Mean?	252
Why Is Truth Important?	255
Wondrous Ways Of Light Workers/Way Showers: A Divine Discussion	262

Y
	266
Your Cosmic Mother: At The Valentine Vortex Of Love	267
Your Star, Your Sun, Your Destiny	271

A Life Divinely Defined					277

Source Listing Of Articles

Adama

Adama's Message	39
Sacred Trilogy Of Teachings	167
Seven Sacred Flames: How To Use Them	168
Seven Sacred Flames: Daily Use	182
Sacred Shifts To Ascend	184
Seven Sacred Steps For Ascension	188
Seven Sacred Flames Chart	191
The Cause And Cure For Terrorism	222

Akashic Records

Changing Your Comprehension Of Change	84
Considering Karma	95
Ever Lasting Energy	113
Our Role In Healing	149
The Divine Gift Of Dreams	229

Akhenaten/Moses & The Great White Brotherhood

Akhenaten/Moses And Me	43

Multi-Archangel Realms

Wondrous Ways Of Light Workers/Way Showers: A Divine Discussion	262
Archangels Gabriel And Raphael	50

Archangel Uriel

A Conversation With Creation	2
A New Future, Five Fundamental Shifts	27
Being Human	82
Competition	94
How To Quickly Change Your World	119
Human Cosmic Construct	120
Knowing Rather Than Seeking	126
Me Or We, You Choose	134
Nine Necessities: Agreeing To Be Human	138
No Failure	140
Rest In Peace 3-D	162
Seven Aspects Of Ascension	193

Some Ways To Love More	214
Spirituality And/Or Religion	215
The Year Of The Starseed, 2016	245
What Does New Mean?	252

Ascended Master Energies

At Present	64

Beings Of Cosmic Consciousness

Coming Home To Your BEingness	88

Christ Consciousness Energy

Religions And Christ Consciousness	156

Council Of Creation

Council Of Creation	99

Cosmic Keepers Of Creation

Creating Community With Creation	104
Only Oneness Omits Isolation	142
The Meaning Of Life	234
Your Star, Your Sun, Your Destiny	271

Cosmic Keepers Of The Akashic Records

Accessing The Akashic Records	32

Cosmic Mother

Your Cosmic Mother: At The Valentine Vortex Of Love	267

Council Of Archangelic Realms (CAR)

Eight Sacred Principles Of Leadership	111
Living Parallel Lives	128
Separating From Separation Into Oneness	208
Ten Tenets Of BEingness: Cosmic Commandments	220

Council Of The Galactic Federations

The Returning Of Oneness	240

Galactic Federation Of Worlds

A New Creation Story	4

I AM Presence And Christ Consciousness Energies

Twelve Codes Of Consciousness	249

Mother Earth

Summer Solstice Letter	217

Phillip Elton Collins

Being A Channel Of Higher Realms	67
I AM: And So Are You!	123
Resurrection: Christ Consciousness Energy (Transcending All Beliefs Into Cosmic Truth)	163
The Gift Of Commitment	233
Why Is Truth Important?	255

Saint Francis

Saint Francis Energy	195

Your Creator

Being Co-Creator: From Child To Adult	76

PREFACE

By Joel Anastasi

Spiritual Journalist, Angel News Network Co-Founder

Wow! Not a very sophisticated way to begin a Preface for a spiritual book, perhaps, but that is my honest reaction to Phillip's latest book documenting the spiritual wisdom that channels through him from so many wonderful higher realm sources.

Phillip seems to produce brilliant spiritual books at the speed some great chefs produce wonderful cuisine. It seems just yesterday I wrote the Preface for his book, *Man Power God Power*, published in 2013. In that preface I wrote, Phillip's book contained an "astonishing compendium of divine wisdom that he personally channeled. If there is a more comprehensive source of teachings available from the higher dimensions, I have not seen it."

Then he published *Activate Your Soul Plan* in 2014, which, in my view, seemed to eclipse *Man Power God Power* in its depth and breadth. Now comes *Divine Discussions*: Higher Realms Speaking Directly To Us, which contains a truly breathtaking range of wisdom all designed, as Archangel Uriel says in his introduction, to assist in mankind's ascension and in the creation of our seventh and final golden age.

The wisdom here pours forth from Adama, the father of humanity, three Archangels, the Akashic Records, and a host of Ascended Master energies many of which you may never have heard of. Once you read what they have to say, you will see for yourself how blessed humankind is to have a powerful cosmic support system beyond our comprehension.

These higher realms tell us mankind has ascended and then crashed and burned through six previous golden ages. Gabriel once told me in preparation for writing my book, *The Second Coming, The Archangel Gabriel Proclaims a New Age*, if mankind didn't get its act together, so to speak, we could crash and burn again. With the assistance of the powerful spiritual energies documented here, it is my great hope and belief that mankind's Ascension into the fifth dimension will be achieved.

How? Read all about it right here. Once again, thank you, Phillip.

Joel D. Anastasi

IN GRATITUDE

When I receive messages from higher realms and write them down I am rarely ever able to see them again within our three dimensional (3D) context. I can mostly see them in the higher frequency from whence they came. Thus, I am in constant need of others to make sure my written words are clear and make sense in our 3D world. I am so blessed to have a group of people who assist me. Since the creation of any book requires many people's talents and gifts coming together, I am especially grateful for the following people who were particularly involved in this latest project:

Sharon Ann Meyer, (AKA, SAM), took this entire manuscript and acted as a 'muse' throughout the entire publication process including editing, formatting and design. Through being a multi-talented messenger herself, she brought untold gifts to this endeavor.

Joel Dennis Anastasi, one of my partners and co-founders within The Angel News Network, a friend and colleague for over 40 years, thank you for the Preface and your continuous support and professional writing eye within all my writings.

Jeff Fasano, my soul brother and co-founder within The Angel News Network, delivered my invitation to channel, making this book and many other teachings and tools from higher realms evident within this Earth reality. He himself is a gifted trance channel, inspiring all channels, and bringing needed wisdoms, truths and tools into humanity.

Omar Prince, actor, writer and social media publicist, thank you for the passion and commitment you bring to the higher realms throughout each and every day. Another keen set of eyes always assisting me.

James Robert Gozon, my husband who creates an unconditionally loving relationship and home where I can write and create in total peace. Many thanks also for constantly rescuing me from my technical deficiencies. None of my seven books could have been published without your caring.

INTRODUCTION

We are all designed and destined to be channels of higher realms, to become multi-dimensional, communicating directly with frequencies and consciousness beyond the human mind, bringing that wisdom into humanity. It has always been this way. We have never been alone and we are not alone now!

All our modern miracles and advancements and all our past 'golden ages' be they Lemurian, Atlantean, Egyptian, Greek, Aztec, Mayan and many others were all supported and created by higher realms wisdom beyond the human experience. We are just beginning to again realize and accept this truth at present. Connecting with higher realms on a regular basis will be a game changer within our existence and greatly affect the future choices we make as a human species.

Let us entertain the thought that the human mind can be a receiver (not originator) of these higher wisdoms, if we so choose, through our freedom of choice and will. I acknowledge accepting wisdom beyond the human mind can be a challenge for some. Please allow the wisdom contained within this book to be testament of that which I speak. My human mind could have never created the wisdom contained within this book. As in all matters in life, use your resonance (how you feel about it with your heart) and discernment (how you think about it with your mind) with what is presented here. I am not attempting to convince nor control anyone. But if you cannot accept the source, focus on the wisdom and see if you can accept its intention to help you. If you can accept the wisdom, and the source, that is the beginning or continuation of a divine connection.

Later within this book, I explain how I became a channel of higher realms and how you can be and do the same. (See "Being A Channel Of Higher Realms" on page 67).

The topics within this book are vast and sometimes revolutionary in thought. There is everything from "A New Creation Story" to divinely discussing the areas within our lives that need to change in order for us to survive and prosper as a planet and species. Again, the intention of these words is to love and support us, not to intend any harm. **Are we ready to receive this?**

Presently, on a regular basis, my Angel News Network colleagues and I facilitate live/teleconference gatherings at The Center For Spiritual Living, Ft. Lauderdale called *Divine Discussions* (Visit PhillipEltonCollins.com and look under the EVENTS tab for information, including audio files of past events.). During these gatherings we bring in the higher realms messages and allow individuals to directly connect to these *higher bands of consciousness* with their questions and received messages. We also have a weekly radio show where I connect with higher realms for their higher realm perspective on current events. This brings me great joy for I know this is an essential aspect of my Divine Soul Plan, my reason to be here.

Glance through the Alphabetical Content and Content By Source pages, see if any one topic and/or source resonates or appeals to you, and go from there...

Even though highly trained as a marketing professional, I am consciously choosing that people find this material through their own resonance, discernment and synchronicity. While I have also partnered and worked with some of the most well-known, successful film, corporate and metaphysical/spiritual individuals, I do not seek their validation or endorsement. This endeavor is for your soul plan to discover. Finally, there will be no submission of these tools and teachings for any award or prize. The reward is you receiving these higher realms wisdoms with grace and ease as an essential aspect of your soul plan.

Having had a rewarding career working with some very gifted/talented people such as my colleagues at **Young & Rubicam Advertising,** New York City, **George Lucas, Steve Jobs and Ridley Scott,** I have also written several books based upon channeled wisdoms. I am forever astounded at the unlimited higher realm gifts *beyond my experiences* presented to us (knowing none of it came from me but through me). If you so choose, through resonance and discernment see if you can receive a wisdom and/or message that has been waiting for you to discover.

The Light Of Source Never Fails,

Phillip Elton Collins

Light Ascension Therapist & Co-Founder of The Angel News Network

PhillipEltonCollins.com

TheAngelNewsNetwork.com

Alphabetical Listing Of Articles: A

A Conversation With Creation
A New Creation Story
A New Future, Five Fundamental Shifts
Accessing The Akashic Records
Adama's Message
Akhenaten/Moses And Me
Archangels Gabriel And Raphael
At Present

A Conversation With Creation

From: Archangel Uriel, World Teacher And Guardian.

Dear Beloved Humans Being Human,

One of the most important conversations you are having is the silent one with yourself, not the ones you are projecting out into the world through your ego masks and defenses.

Take a deep breath and check in with that silent talk with self. Are you judging and shaming yourself in unspoken words? Is that silent conversation balancing with the one you are giving out into the world? Or are the two conversations decidedly different? Are you saying one thing outwardly and really feeling and saying another inside?

Dear ones, that silent talk is your true feeling about yourself. It is also a *conversation with Creation*. Once you are able to take a deep examination of that silent self-talk you can grasp a handle on what exactly needs to heal and be released within self; a process of inside out, not outside in.

If it resonates, throughout your day periodically check in with yourself and, without judgment nor shame of self, take a deep breath and truly listen to what you are saying about you to you. Is it loving and accepting with compassion, thus forgiving how you are choosing to learn what you need to learn, the way you need to learn it? Also realize, dear ones, this cozy conversation does not stop within you. The energy from this self-talk resonates out into your world and beyond. It actually affects how others resonate with you. Like-kind vibrations/frequencies (The Law of Attraction) attract one another. So, if you truly feel non-loving of self, spoken or not, this is what you will create in your life and will send out to the forces of Creation since everything is interconnected.

Learning to lovingly check in with your silent self-talk is a powerful tool to become more aware/conscious of self in order to release unhealed aspects of self and to allow making another choice through your freedom of will.

DIVINE DISCUSSIONS

A New Creation Story

From: Galactic Federation of Worlds.

*Y*ou *will know the truth and the truth will set you free,* has echoed throughout the ages within your spiritual wisdoms. Now beloved humans of the beautiful planet Earth, we of the *Galactic Federation of Worlds* come to you at this time of ascension on your planet *to paint* another view of yourselves: *where you truly came from* that will allow you to more truthfully know where you are divinely headed. As with all truth and wisdom (applied knowledge), you will discern through your freedom of choice and will what resonates and what does not.

Who Is The *Galactic Federation Of Worlds*?

We, the *Galactic Federation of Worlds*, are an immense federation of civilizations from a diverse range of planets, galaxies and multiverses working together (Unity Consciousness) for the harmonious existence of all life (your Divine Destiny). The Galactic Federation for your Milky Way Galaxy is located in the Sirius Star Systems. Your sun is a star gate to that system. The Milky Way Galaxy Galactic Federation is the oldest Galactic Federation in this Universe. It was established at the end of the first Great Galactic War that was fought in the Lyra Constellation (the original Lyran home of the messenger we are coming through now, and the reason his soul plan includes revealing the following truth with you) between the beings we shall later discuss in this message. The supposedly fictional **Star Wars** stories reflect much of what actually happened. Our messenger at this time had an extensive film career with the divine soul who brought these 'open-heartedly-received–stories' to humanity. *Now you humans, through the present ascension energies, advancement of your sciences, consciousness, and communication abilities, are ready to receive the truth as the truth. The following creation story could not have been imagined or accepted earlier.*

There is much history and details of our *Galactic Federation of Worlds* available to you, but we do not wish to overload you with the vast names and events at this time; know that each race, civilization and planet has a council within the *Galactic Federation of Worlds* to represent them. Suffice to say, for the information about to be shared, the *Galactic Federation of Worlds has grown and become a very empowering federation of worlds devoted to universal peace and prosperity, which you are in the process of achieving on this planet. This message is to support that process.*

How The Past Affects The Present

It is the intention of this body of truth and wisdom for you to know the truth that will set you free from your past and present. **Much of your present genetic coding/DNA configuration has to do with your often unknown origins.** Your lack of love within duality, attempting to control one another, confrontation and killing, has been passed on for eons. The Ascension Process of your planet along with the awareness/consciousness of your past will assist in the healing and positive alteration of your present. If you so choose, it is time to heal the past that has factored into the present for generations. **This rather new creation story for many does not discount your Divinity or a loving creator who has factored in your freedom of** choice and will as learning tools. Accept with compassion, forgive with no judgment and take ownership of how you have chosen to learn what you need to learn. All of this is a Divine Ascension Process of you and your planet moving into a higher frequency of existence.

This information has always existed for any and all who have been ready to receive it. In fact, all of what we are about to share exists within many of the ancient documents that have been hidden or have been or are about to be revealed to the masses. There are billions of you on this planet now and the only way you have been controlled has been through **deceit and secrecy**. As you increase your awareness, more of you than ever before desire peace and equality but there are often hidden forces of power wishing to keep control. Again, the information sharing within this message is to assist in your freedom of creating a world of true equality, harmony and balance. *We urge you to set aside all drama attached to conspiracy theories and know the truth.* There are many messengers bringing you the truth now; use your resonance and discernment to know what is true for you.

Knowledge is indeed power. It is time within your Ascension Process, if you so choose, to desire true freedom, to speak the truth, express your needs and set your boundaries against non-truth. It is time to make another choice in regard to those who wish to control your world through fear and duality. War and religion were successfully used as separation-control tools in the past. Now with nuclear weapons that can destroy much of your planet war is no longer an option. There has been almost complete destruction in the past, which we shall discuss later. With religion not holding the power it once did, the power of money and **controlling economics and cyber war are the new methods to attempt to control people, usually through hidden forces.** As we have a universal view, we see you are in process with creating new criteria for selecting those who govern your world. The higher realms of Creation have sent you many teachings and tools to assist in your mastery of self and freedom that can reflect into manifesting a new world paradigm of unity consciousness. *Often the messenger has been quieted or killed by prevailing forces. Are you ready to receive and apply the given tools now?*

It is the further intention of this message to shine a great bright, white light upon the vast and ancient powers of often hidden, other- world- beings and humans of an unthinkable/unbelievable power-elite whose mission has been to control and stop the divine ascension of humanity (long before your recorded religious or spiritual histories). It is your destiny to activate your soul plans (reason to be here) through truth and once and for all become free. You have simply chosen this way to learn what you need to learn -- that you are eternal Divine Beings Of Light intended to be in world and universal service for the good of all.

Dear humans, as we share the forthcoming *new story of creation*, please know telling the truth is a way **to break the codes of secrecy that have controlled your world.** By knowing what those controlling powers *think* their possibilities are, you can free yourself from them. They plan to continue to accumulate all the power and wealth they can (a small percentage already controls the vast majority of your wealth and power). They have the intention of continuing contact with ancient *advanced being creators*. In some cases, they have been in contact with advanced civilizations and are being guided and in some cases controlled by them. Some who control you now are the *original ancient creators of humanity*. As quantum physics/mechanics has proven, your awareness of all this will shift and change it. *Human beings are not destined to be a slave race lost on a paradise planet in a small galaxy.* How you began does not dictate where you end up, dear humans. *From seemingly humble beginnings extraordinary things can and do grow; from a seed of an advanced civilization, you are destined to create your own mighty BEingness, and ascend from whence you came.* You have already advanced more in the last one hundred years than in the past one thousand years, and it is speeding up even faster.

We realize that what is now explained may be very challenging for some. If it resonates, please allow this story to unfold, and at the end of it, through your resonance and discernment, know what is true for you.

Humanity is a divine aspect of an advanced civilization that is in the process of fully awakening to its own Divine Soul Plan to manifest the reason you came into existence: to become the master teachers of this world and beyond. This is the reason you chose the path of creation you did. It is all in perfect *Divine Order* no matter how it may appear (your world at present is filled with old DNA upheaval that you are in the process of clearing and cleansing, and you are awakening new spiritual DNA that will facilitate your destiny).

None of what is related previously, or about to be related, denies the existence of a universal all loving creative God Power, a BEingness of all energy and existence. *The awareness of this one God Power, that created all that created you, wishes you to remember there is more to life than this three dimensional material existence, and all you are experiencing now is a preparation to move into that higher frequency of BEing to be in service to it all.*

Another Explanation For The Creation And Origin Of This Planet And Its Human People

Beloved humans, whom we have been observing since the beginning of your creation, please remember and know that all we are about to share also exists in many of your ancient documents, particularly from the Sumerian culture since they had a form of clay tablet writing which has been preserved into your present time. Many of the mysteries revealed concerning your creation began in Mesopotamia between the Tigris and Euphrates rivers. It is interesting to note that the Sumerians were located in what you now call southern Iraq where you have so little access due to current conflicts. The records of what happened are recorded and preserved in cuneiform clay tablet writings and during the past 100 plus years have slowly been revealed to you. The Sumerian culture seemed to appear from nothing, lasted two thousand years and then vanished.

The Sumerians received (from an advanced civilization) what appeared many 'firsts' for your world such as: (1) the first writing system; (2) the wheel; (3) creation of educational institutions; (4) development of history; (5) a code of laws; (6) governmental structure; (7) taxation; (8) astronomy, knowing the cosmos thousands of years ahead of other cultures; (9) metal money; (10)

social sciences and reforms. How did a civilization that lasted 2,000 years do this as well as 'create' sixty minutes in an hour and advanced cosmic calendars beyond present wisdom?

The one thing that all your ancient cultures believed in were gods who had descended to Earth from the heavens above and could come and go at will. Now that humanity has begun to explore outer space and astronauts are preparing to land on other worlds, it is not impossible for your world today to believe that a civilization from another planet more advanced than yours is capable of having been here or still is here.

Dear humans, when you read the Sumerian tablets you quickly learn they never considered those who brought them knowledge as 'gods.' This only happened later in your history with the Egyptians, Greeks and Romans. Sumerians called them "*Those Who Came To Earth From Heaven*" or "Anunnaki." Your Old Testament *Bible* speaks of *ancient heroes* who were products of sexual relations with heavenly beings and human women. There is a constant theme and concept running throughout human recorded history that during the planet's ancient past, *advanced beings from other civilizations came to this planet and affected the evolution of humanity*. There are many structures remaining today from this past that you do not have the technology to build nor fully understand. It is your destiny for this to change.

A New History

This is the Galactic Federation's history we wish to share supported by ancient Sumerian literature. More than four billion years ago, a roaming, rogue planet called

Nibiru entered your solar system crashing into another large planet bombarding the other planet with its many moons. These particles created what you call your asteroid belt while the other half of the planet was knocked into a new orbit closer to your sun. These fragments over eons coalesced into your planet Earth. One of Nibiru's moons became your own moon. This information explains why your planet is missing much of its crust and the origin of your asteroid belt. The waters from these colliding planets created your oceans.

As you know, life on planet Earth is based upon one-year cycles around your sun, one solar 365-day calendar year. Life on Nibiru was based on a one-year orbit around the sun of 3,800 Earth years, allowing life to evolve sooner than on Earth. The difference in the two planet's timetables/life spans explains how one world could be perceived by the other as immortal. Your short-lived insects see the human life span the same way.

During Earth's second major ice age, when the two planets came closer together again, the advanced civilization of Nibiru made a water landing on planet Earth (not unlike your astronauts of today).

Thus, almost 500,000 years ago an advanced galaxy-galloping-group of humanoid cosmic beings found their way to Planet Earth. From Sumerian readings these beings came from a *twelfth much larger planet* in your solar system they named Nibiru. Since the Sumerians had already identified all the planets in this solar system, and they counted your moon and sun, they arrived at the number twelve.

As with your present day astronauts these ancient spacemen needed to find a base camp, which offered a source of water, fuel and decent weather. Mesopotamia (southern Iraq, which still offers these today) met their needs. The Nile and Indus Rivers offered backups. It is interesting to note that the places where these initial world visits took place are still largely inaccessible today due to human conflict. More wisdom lies there to discover.

The advanced peoples the Sumerians called the Anunnaki began an organized colonization of Earth. Later, in relationship with *human subjects,* they would assume the role of 'gods.' Being advanced beings did not prevent disagreements and divisions amongst the Anunnaki and affected much of their behavior. Over thousands of Earth years, but only a few years to the Anunnaki, an established colony of these 'space pirates' was set, and they began to focus on their purpose in coming to Earth: to mine Earth's mineral wealth, especially gold for use on their home planet. Just like humans today, the Anunnaki had damaged their planet's ozone layer and needed micro-flakes of gold to repair their upper atmosphere. Scientists on Earth recently discovered that minute gold flakes are the best way to heal Earth's atmosphere. At present, proof of ancient mining has been revealed from the Persian Gulf to (South) Africa, to South and Central America. The Anunnaki mining efforts were worldwide and can explain the early diffusion of humans. There remain today ancient 'cave paintings' of this time.

Spaceships, from vast Earth distances, transported raw mined ore back to Mesopotamia for processing; engraving of the gold ingots is numerous in archeological digs around the fore mentioned areas. Problems eventually arose amongst the Anunnaki due to the laborious efforts needed to mine and process, not to mention some extreme climate shifts that were taking place on the maturing Earth.

After some 100,000 years of body-breaking mining themselves, the Anunnaki realized they needed to create another way to obtain Earth's gold and other minerals. Their scientists huddled and agreed; they needed to create a primitive worker called an *Adama.* Today you can find remains of a Homo erectus humanoid in the mining areas earlier mentioned. **The High Councils of the Anunnaki approved what became the genetic manipulation of an existing species, not the creation of a new race.** With the scientific knowledge (cloning) you have today, you can fully understand this. Earlier in your history, no one could have accepted what we explain here.

The First Test Tube Babies

Through laboratory experimentation, many mutated creatures (such as the sphinx -- half humanoid, half lion) were created (the basis for some of your mythological creatures and super humans). Experimentation with an *existing primitive African female hominoid* and the sperm of a young male Anunnaki eventually created a humanoid. The fertilized ovum was then placed inside a female Anunnaki for the pregnant term. This produced a healthy young male Adama hybrid for the first time on Earth, bypassing the concept of evolution. Dear humans of today, these early humans behaved more like animals with a shorter life span than their creators, and were unable to reproduce (the Anunnaki feared future competition from this new human being; little did they know what was to come from their creation!) Anunnaki then went on to produce a series of non-reproductive Adamas, male and female. These Adamas were the first test tube babies.

Adamas were not destined for lives of grace and ease but lives of toil at the hands of their 'gods.' The ancient humans saw the Anunnaki as gods since they possessed super powers and seemed to live forever. Slavery in human life has been common from the first known civilizations until now. The concept of slavery became imprinted in human DNA and has been passed on for human generations to this day. The *word 'worship' is a mistranslation of the 'work-ship'. These ancient humans did not worship their gods; they worked for them.*

Know, dear humans, while the Anunnaki had seemingly little compassion for the plight of humans, they eventually did decide to grant humans their first Sumerian civilization after further adjusting of the human genetic code and an unsuccessful attempt to exterminate all human life. What the Anunnaki did not realize is that the upper human genetic code is sacred, and they could never have full access to it. Only the Creator who created that code has full access.

How Humans Came To Reproduce

As humans today have often treated work animals without compassion, the Anunnaki treated the first humans the same. Since these early humans were prevented from reproducing (because Anunnaki had a fear of them taking over), new individuals had to be produced all the time. The in vitro fertilization and birthing process was time and labor consuming. It was decided that the Adama-race would have to reproduce itself in order to be more productive and labor efficient. Anunnaki created a human reproductive lab to further manipulate the genetic code to allow sexual reproduction. This procedure involved obtaining life-affirming Adama DNA; male Adama DNA combined with a female Adama rather than an Anunnaki, (through DNA sequence splicing, a procedure within your technology today).

The successful result was a male Adama who could reproduce with a female Adama through sexual intercourse. Continued DNA manipulation reduced the human life span (even though through Anunnaki DNA, the humans lived much longer than you do today) and mental body capacities. Now that the human population could grow on its own, the Adamas were transported to the far-reaching mining operations throughout the globe. **This explains human expansion throughout the world.** As a result of human expansion, reproductive capacity, and closer contact with the Anunnaki, there began some interbreeding (changing Neanderthal to Cro-Magnon), and some Adamas even escaped.

Remember, the early Adamas had many of the Anunnaki genes, thus they lived thousands of years but much less than the Anunnaki. This human life span slowly declined as interbreeding continued and the consequences of life on planet Earth had their effect. But the much longer life spans of pure Anunnaki ruler/masters allowed them to continue to appear immortal. Anti-aging technology even further increased Anunnaki life spans.

Within your timelines, the first human Adamas were produced some three hundred thousand years ago. As mentioned, after additional genetic manipulation, Anunnaki males began interbreeding with human women some one hundred thousand years ago. As planet Earth continued to mature, a new ice age dramatically reduced the human population (not even the Anunnaki could control this).

What you call Neanderthal vanished while the so called Cro-Magnon survived solely in what is now the Middle East. Your present science confirms this.

Humans fathered by Anunnaki with human women were eventually allowed to govern in controlled and selected cities (some fifty thousand years ago). Many ancient civilizations reflect this evolution that came and went. Not all Anunnaki thought this a good idea; thus, internal disagreement and discontent grew.

Weather Changes, Wars & Noah's Ark

Mother Earth continued her dramatic weather shifts (some twelve thousand years ago) and the Anunnaki knew the soon return of their home planet Nibiru's orbit (gravitational pull) would compound these severe weather patterns. This advanced race would not be able to continue their mission on Earth for the moment. *It is important to note again the Anunnaki were not the only advanced civilizations on Earth. Extraterrestrials had come and gone on this planet for eons. This particular period was also the late Lemurian and Atlantean eras (more on this later).*

The Anunnaki had no other choice but to wait out Earth weather events in their evacuation spaceships orbiting the planet. The majority of the governing Anunnaki planned to allow the weather to destroy the humans since they felt the entire experiment had grown out of hand. But not all agreed. Generations of intermarriage created family connections, and some had come to love their creation.

ALPHABETICAL LISTING OF ARTICLES: A

Many of humanity's histories/religions note 'flood stories' as well as creation stories. If it resonates, you can accept or not accept the following flood story. Most of your flood stories are a version of what actually happened.

Certain forces wished to save what had been created, since some Anunnaki developed affection for their human creations and were genetically connected to them, and some began to love. There was a construct of an ark but it was not to actually have a live specimen of each species. Some of those who had been involved in the genetic engineering of humans took DNA samples of all living things, rather than an ark-load of live beings; thus, the ark was filled with scientific vials. This was much easier to transport and insured survival since no one knew how long the weather conditions would prevail. The Anunnaki who represented 'Noah' and three ethnically different surrogate wives produced three sons to represent the various races of the world. Those who were curious about the ark building were told the samples would be taken back to the home planet for future enslavement. But the true secret of the plan to save humanity for Earth was successfully kept from the 'master-gods,' the Anunnaki.

The 'Great Flood' was not solely the result of heavy rains. Because of the returned planetary pull of the large planet Nibiru, hurricane force winds and darkness from erupting volcanoes prevailed. There was worldwide catastrophe, but not all parts of planet Earth were under water, even though the Nibiru gravitational pull caused polar ice sheets to slip into the oceans, raising sea levels everywhere. Even now, most of the original Anunnaki cities in Mesopotamia remain deep under water waiting for your further discovery.

DIVINE DISCUSSIONS

After many days of heavy storm events things began to settle down, but still no land was seen. A short while later the ark landed atop a mountain, as the water continued to recede. As Noah and his family began to leave the ark, they drew the attention of the returning Anunnaki circling the planet. It was not in the Divine Soul Plan of humans to be destroyed but a choice they had made in higher realms to be 'created' this way. Confronted by the reality that humans survived, and perhaps feeling some karmic remorse for past actions, the Anunnaki chose to relent and further permit human expansion and growth on planet Earth.

This flood story explains the sudden absence of a large portion of the human population some ten thousand years ago due to the Great Flood echoed in almost all your ancient histories. With the flood waters continuing to lower and planet Nibiru moving further out of the solar system, the Anunnaki and a (divinely) chosen group of remaining humans set about creating a new world.

Creating A New World But Not Better

Since the Anunnaki (and humans) had not yet evolved into a peaceful, loving culture, the post flood world was even less peaceful than the previous one. *These non-peaceful, non-loving aspects of self remain within your DNA today and are in the process of evolving and healing.* **This message may assist you in understanding current events in your world at present.**

A majority of humans worked directly for the Anunnaki before the flood; remaining humans were nomadic hunter-gatherers. The post flood changed the landscape, forcing humans to transition into farmers. This explains the sudden appearance of certain artificially manipulated food crops (never seen before) some thirteen thousand years ago. *This reshaped all the rest of human history.* Humans began to cultivate the land and domesticate animals because they were forced to do so. This was a strategy by the Anunnaki to survive remaining on the planet until they could resume mining its natural resources. With farming and plenty to eat (the flood had created rich soil) came the concentration of people in villages and cities much larger and more complex than before the flood.

Each new city was ruled by an Anunnaki official, being considered a 'god' by the humans. In addition to 'godship' over humans, agriculture and animals, the Anunnaki began to allow and grant leadership to certain humans. As humans grew in numbers, the Anunnaki knew they had to take measures to maintain control over their creation (this control factor is also in human DNA today). It was decided to split up the human population within three geographical locations: Mesopotamia and the Nile and Indus Valleys. The Sinai Peninsula, the new Anunnaki space flight command, was a non-human, holy, sacred place. Please pay attention to how your past history and current events continue to take place in these three areas.

Birth Of Kingdoms And Royal Lineage

Now that humans were in various locations and building communities, separate leaders were needed. Thus the concept of 'kingdoms' (human rulers chosen by the Anunnaki or 'gods' to represent them) were created. *The structure of dynastic kingships/kingdoms based on a royal lineage traceable to the gods was born.* Think how this has dramatically affected the development of countries, governments and religions to this day. This practice began the Sumerian civilization and affected the Egyptian, Aztec and Mayan and others later as well as the Lemurian and Atlantean before these. Again, it is worth noting that the Anunnaki were not the only space visitors on Earth; the planet had many beings from many worlds throughout its history. We are focusing on the original creation of the planet itself and the Anunnaki involvement for this message.

Tower Of Babel, Great Pyramids, And Sphinx

The name Mesopotamia is a combination of ancient words that connotes the idea of a 'vehicle that flies up'. The Tower of Babel actually was not about language or names but a launching pad for spaceships. The true story is that humans at one point attempted to build their own spaceship tower, launch pad to rebel against their rulers and to determine their own fate. This increased the Anunnaki desire to break up (disperse) the humans even more and destroy any such tower. Through the further relocations of humans at the hands of the Anunnaki, different languages did develop over eons of time. Humans were taken by advanced transportation systems to Africa, Asia, Arabia, Indus Valley and the near East to do the bidding of the Anunnaki, as mining of Earth's resources resumed. Again, there are ancient cave paintings depicting this.

Peace was possible with the further dispersion of humanity as new communities, cities (kingdoms), and food supply increased, but, alas, the Anunnaki ancient gods were no more able to maintain and sustain peace any more than you humans are today. Now you know where it came from within yourselves.

Remember, flood waters were continuing to recede, and many of the earlier Anunnaki space flight and other facilities were still under water. These *ancient gods* were constantly looking for natural landmarks and sites to build telecommunication/energy centers and launching stations for their space travel needs. **Twin peaks of the two great pyramids of Giza were built for such needs.** The Sphinx was the central control center for the pyramids. Even though the great pyramids (and Sphinx) have long been de-activated from their original electro-magnetic force fields and side shields and gold capstones removed, modern day astronauts confirm the pyramids still serve as a beacon and radar reflector from outer space. This powerful reflector served as a 'lighthouse' for approaching space ships and still does! You can use your own reasoning as for the existence and purpose of pyramids in other cultures throughout your world's history. Many of these structures in a reduced state still exist, and their mysteries await your discovery. **The truth of your history will further allow you to create a new world of equality, harmony and balance...to set you free from your past.**

Further Meaning Of The Moon

The ancient and lost meaning of the word 'sin' is moon. Remember, your moon was one of the planet Nibiru's moons when it crashed into another planet (Tiamat). This moon also contained organic material used in the hybrid creation of humans in the Anunnaki experiments. This material still exists in your moon today, and it is your destiny to learn how to harvest it for the good of humanity. When some of your religious historians came along, they reiterated the story that you were born in 'sin'. They were correct in that statement but conveniently left out the fact that *sin* referred to *Moon*, one of the sources of your genetic material/makeup. *This was the beginning of organized religions judging, shaming and blaming humanity in order to control you.*

New History Continues

By the time all the repair work was completed from the great flood, new generations of Anunnaki were actually born on Earth; remember the long life spans of these people that was far greater than humans. Just because the Anunnaki were technologically advanced did not mean that their Ascension Process into Unity Consciousness was complete. Like a script out of one of your science fictions movies, such as **Star Wars** or **Avatar**, there were many civil wars, and conspiracies, brother against brother, sister against sister (like your American Civil War). See the pattern of repetition passed on! These confrontations and rebellions eventually involved humans, thus providing the first human exposure to lethal combat, which is continuing as we speak.

From this point on some of your history is accurate with many missing details. As stated earlier there were many space- faring beings on the planet during this time. Each of them, including the Anunnaki, influenced other advanced Earth civilizations such as Lemuria (to learn more about Lemuria see this messenger's book: *Coming Home To Lemuria, An Ascension Adventure Story*) and Atlantis. The Anunnaki were very involved in the creation of the ten island Atlantean civilization located in the Atlantic Ocean. The destruction of Atlantis was due to their extreme power abuse (tactical nuclear weapons) that threatened the survival of planet Earth. From Atlantis what we know as Egypt was created. Since

Egypt is better known to humanity today, we shall continue to focus on it rather than Lemuria and Atlantis. From Atlantis, one of the major Anunnaki leaders gained sovereignty over what became Egypt and was known as Ra. Ra's children created the lineage for future pharaohs by marrying each other. Thus, famous rulers such as Osiris, Isis, and Seth came to be. Much family rivalry and wars with outsiders were passed down from earlier times. Armed conflict, beginning with rivalries and intrigues between Anunnaki god-kings, were fought by mind-controlled human subjects who were under required religious obedience to the Anunnaki. All this was quite successful in keeping the unaware, unconscious humans in control. **The names may be hidden and have changed, but this is still going on today. It is time to wake up, if you so choose.**

The intermarriage of Anunnaki and humans continued, and there were many family feuds and civil disputes experienced over the years that have been echoed in much of humanity's classic literature such as the Greek god epics and 'Romeo and Juliet' tales. The divine DNA aspects of the humans, which the Anunnaki could never access, continued to awaken, and their quest for freedom and power grew. With the help of sympathetic Anunnaki, another human hybrid was also created and supported by higher realms and beings, such as pharaoh **Akhenaten/Moses** (this messenger also has a karmic incarnational connection to the channel). **Akhenaten/Moses** came into being to receive higher consciousness energy to further support the evolution/ascension of humanity into its Eternal Oneness (a process that is continuing today).

The Anunnaki became even more threatened by humans

and employed nuclear weaponry again. This was the second nuclear blast the planet endured. This occurred before the year 2,000 B.C. Your Earth rocks still contain the radioactivity of this event. Today humanity does not know how to handle/store the manipulation of one of the universe's most powerful energy sources, nuclear energy. The divine energy within nuclear power was never intended for destruction but for construction through love. *This corrupted use of Creation's energy, through the unhealed Anunnaki DNA, is an essential aspect of humanity that is in the process of healing through the activation of spiritual DNA, which the Anunnaki could not shut down*. Never forget you are all Divine Beings on a sacred journey to servicing your world and universe. You are learning 'what is' through 'what is not,' your choice through your freedom of will.

And Along Came Abraham

At this junction in human history, the biblical patriarch called Abraham incarnated (Divine Destiny of humanity). Abraham was much more than someone wandering in the wilderness. He was a high-ranking Sumerian who met with pharaoh's court, made treaties, commanded troops to free humans from Anunnaki control and stopped their advancement in other areas. Abraham's god Yahweh (God of the Mountains), and a loyal Anunnaki, kept in communication with his chosen (human) people through a radio transmitter-receiver otherwise known as the **Ark** *of the Covenant.* ***The Ten Commandments*** *received by Moses were placed inside as the power source to activate the Ark,* whose code the Anunnaki could not break. The nuclear blast, described above (2,000 B.C.), was an Anunnaki reaction to this behavior. The story of Sodom and Gomorrah echoed this nuclear explosion turning flesh into a pillar of salt, nuclear vaporized. Abraham, many miles away, witnessed this extraordinary misuse of energy. Surrounding villages were abandoned for several centuries (2,050 B.C.). Today the fresh water near the Dead Sea still contains harmful levels of radioactivity. The Anunnaki used weaker nuclear devices to destroy space launch stations and other equipment in order to keep them from falling into disloyal Anunnaki or human hands. Much of this unnatural scarring of the Sinai Peninsula can be seen from outer space today, as well as burned rocks. The vortex of Sinai still contains the astral Anunnaki energy and continues to release its effects in the world today.

After The Blast

As with nuclear blasts, the aftermath created a radioactive storm, which traveled throughout Mesopotamia killing all life and ending the Sumerian civilization. Standard history cannot explain how such an advanced civilization appeared and disappeared without explanation. For those willing to see the truth, the Sumerian texts tell another terrible tale.

The original Mesopotamian writing recorded the truth. This history was later rewritten to form a base for early religious cults, which became Judaism and later Christianity. The corrupted/adapted new histories were so different from the truth that the truth became mythology or untruths.

With the Anunnaki's nuclear Armageddon in full force and their eons-old 'Garden of Eden' blasted to bits, most decided to return to their home planet, leaving the hybrids and humans behind. To humans all this happened in ancient times, more than four thousand years ago; to the Anunnaki this was just over a year of their life span/time.

Those who survived the blast went through an extreme regression into primitive culture and loss of knowledge. The survivors began recreating a world/civilization without the advancement of their 'gods/masters.' Abraham's people moved far away from the devastation, and with his hybrid genes at one hundred years of age Abraham fathered a son, Isaac. Isaac's son, Jacob, also called Israel, became the name of a people and today a country fighting for its existence within the vortex energy we speak of now. The name, Israel, is a combination of the Egyptian gods Osiris and Ra and the Mesopotamian god EL. After almost forty generations of Israelites, now with a written language, a version of the above was written in Hebrew.

In Conclusion

This is not a complete history of your world but a history of its beginnings. Everything shared here has existed for a long time and been revealed by others. Through resonance and discernment, perhaps more of you will be ready to accept with compassion and forgive how you have all chosen to learn what you needed to learn. After the aforementioned events, the Christ Consciousness energies came into your world through a human being reminding and teaching you how to love one another. Are you ready to receive and be this love and create the true paradise you are meant to be? The United States of America (USA) is destined to support the creation of a new world of Oneness through the creation of the New Jer-USA-lem. (Jerusalem).

A New Future, Five Fundamental Shifts

From: Archangel Uriel, World Teacher And Guardian.

Freedom of choice and will and your Divine Destiny are promised to each of you and integrated in your purpose (soul plan) in being here.

As you approach the end of an old year and head fast into a New Year, let us review some tools and wisdoms from higher realms to assist humanity in creating the world you say you want, knowing you are the creators creating.

If it resonates, let us now open your knowing hearts (moving from your believing minds) to all the possibilities and probabilities of humanity creating a new paradigm, rather than staying resigned to what has been in the past and is currently in the present, knowing "being present is the present."

Within the unseen higher realms, there is an unbroken wholeness, a Divine Order, out of which all events manifest. It is the lost truth of this that has and is creating much of the imbalance in your world. Humanity chose to be an essential aspect of this unbroken/united/integrated Whole (call it what you may). One of the most important roles of humanity is to individually and collectively allow an opening/portal (moving beyond your minds) to receive the Divine Order manifesting. This allows the integration of higher realms with the human soul and spirit and your being into doing.

The integration of higher realms with humanity allows an extraordinary empowering personal process, assisting humanity in feeling and creating new realities. Humans move from children to adults allowing all needs and questions of the child to be fulfilled. In effect, this heals and frees the wounded inner child to become the elevated adult.

Humanity largely bases the conventional view of reality upon positional personal power and ego based accomplishments. But the ascended view of reality is based upon creating a frequency in which humanity constantly expands, grows, and becomes more capable of participating in their unfolding future. This allows the tools of synchronistic nature and marvelous miracles to manifest.

The opportunity and ability to truly participate in your unfolding future has to do with your 'being'; your doing based upon your being, your awakened state of being conscious. So often your lives are based upon doing without knowing neither who you are nor why you are here. Once you have the who and why in place as your foundation, you can build the what, where, when and how.

Creation is a moment by moment domain in which you all constantly deepen your wisdom of reality and choose to participate in creating the future. Then you can individually and collectively see what is needed to emerge in the world and have the compassion and commitment to create what is needed.

Let Us Now Discuss Five Fundamental Shifts Needed To Advance As A Species:

1. How You Think About The World
Planet Earth is a living, conscious being with organs (air, water, minerals, oil, gas, light, etc.) in order to maintain and sustain itself, like yourselves. The ignorance and arrogance of humanity, and how it continues to abuse its very home, is a reflection of how humanity feels about itself. If humanity intends to survive, it is time to

create a new awareness that knows the planet, humanity and the universe is an open, dynamic, integrated organism. What affects one affects all. Once humanity understands and accepts the true reality of their world and the universe, this immediately closes the old doors, locks them, and opens new doors for change and improvement. You know that the future is not fixed and controlled by the few over the many, and as individuals you can shift from resignation to creating the new. What do you choose? Leaders reflect those who choose them.

2. Understanding Relationship

It has been spoken for eons that "the only relationship you are having is the one with self." How you feel and think about yourself is constantly reflected out into your relationships with others and the world. You cannot judge, shame or blame another without first doing this to self. Once you have mastered self, you shall no longer have wounded little boys and girls running the world and often destroying each other and your planet. This is a healing process of inside out, not outside in. In fact, relationship is the organizing principle of the universe. All relationships are reaching inward then outward to all other things. Since you are all dense energy, through interaction with other energy sources, you create. Once you know that relationship is the defining principle of the universe, you can see and accept one another as essential aspects of the Whole. The universe would be incomplete without each of us. The next step is to know you are all one.

3. The Gift Of Commitment (Also See Page 233)

Your readiness for commitment is fundamental to any shift. Many believe that commitment is doing anything in order to succeed. But there is a higher frequency aspect of commitment beyond human will transcending into willingness. This is an inner Divine Voice (aspect of self) that gently guides you through your soul plan (your reason to be here). The key ingredient within this type of commitment is a knowing trust that allows surrender. This surrender (to not knowing) to all possibilities and probabilities allows you to know the fragments within your soul plans, your destiny. It is at this consciousness you shift your relationship with the future. You know and see yourselves as an essential aspect of this world and unfolding future and universe. It is at this point in relationship to self and *All There Is*, this state of BEingness, your life is organically fused with meaning, value and purpose. You release your unhealed self and unfree will to your divine BEingness. At this point, you see the power and gift of commitment.

The moment you fully commit to anything, there is no fear, doubt or ignorance (the monsters of mankind). Once you commit, you move beyond wounds and ego defenses to be and do who you are. Not being who you truly are kills countless manifestations of creation and prevents the elementary truth: You are the Creator creating. Then a pathway clears with grace and ease that no human ever dreamed before. You know your feelings, thoughts and actions are the countenance of Creation, your commitment.

4. *Creating Community*
Once you are able to commit, a cosmic flow of energy (meaning, value and purpose) commences. Through your resonance, communities of equality, harmony and balance begin to form. When you are in a state of surrender, the universal laws of attraction come into play due to the authentic and transparent truth of your BEingness (not because you are special; you are simply

showing the way), and the full possibilities of the future appear. Through commitment and the communities you create, you move from self, to others, to the world and beyond in full service and gratitude for what is (rather than what is not).

5. <u>Synchronicity</u>
At this crucial time in humanity's planetary and human evolution, many universal laws and messages are coming to further support your pathway (such as this one). Understanding synchronicity is one of them. It is no accident or coincidence that this message or the people in your life are there now. The events and people you need in your life now are the very people you need in correlation to your commitment. Old doors close and lock, new doors open, a sense of grace and ease develops and you find you are interacting in a cohesive community of people who may not even be (yet) conscious of one another. In effect, you have moved and are acting from the me to the We in a new paradigm of unity. This is the cosmic wheel of *Divine Order* moving all events forward. Then your lives become a series of non-mindful, marvelous miracles.

In Conclusion

Again, all of the above is a process of inside out, not outside in. The non-mindful, marvelous miracles of life are about your consciousness of character through your being more than your doing. Your world and humanity stand at a vital juncture in your evolutionary path. If you so choose, it is time to free yourselves from yourselves and allow your destiny as Divine Beings to emerge and create a new and glorious future. What do you choose?

DIVINE DISCUSSIONS

Accessing The Akashic Records

From: Cosmic Keepers Of The Akashic Records.

Dear Beloved Humans Being Human,

The Universe is composed of a divine perfected design and order. Your world is also destined to reflect this perfection. At this time we, The Cosmic Keepers Of The Akashic Records, would like to discuss a wonder-filled aspect of the Universe, The Akashic Records. Many have heard this name before. Let us now, through the dispensation of the Ascension Process of your planet and human species, further discuss the meaning, value and purpose of these Records--a mighty tool of Creation!

The Akashic Records are named after the Divine Mother/Feminine Presence energy of Akasha whose mission is to introduce you to the lost knowledge, the "Tree of Life" teachings. Akasha's goal is to awaken you to your true spiritual nature and self. (See this channel's message from the Cosmic Mother on page 267 for more information on this subject) The Sanskrit name/word Akasha means limitless space. The Akashic Records themselves may be further clarified as a divine database that stores everything. All your past and present lives experiences are stored here. Every emotion and thought you have had (creating your reality) is first stored within your planet's atmosphere, creating your weather and natural events and later transferred to The Akashic Records. Every deed and relationship you ever experienced are stored within these routed records for you to access between and during lifetimes for your spiritual growth and expansion. Your freedom of choice and will determines what you choose to apply or not.

ALPHABETICAL LISTING OF ARTICLES: A

The reason for your many incarnational cycles/lifetimes on this planet is to complete the learning stored within The Akashic Records, the God Power Mind.

Let us now describe how you may access The Akashic Records:

Let your mantra be, "I release myself from myself, this is not about me." See yourself transmuting from your physical body to your etheric Light body, which lies just outside you. You now move beyond your personality, wounds and ego defenses. You become aware of a shaft of white light that you intuitively follow. As you move along the shaft of light, you gradually become aware of various chambers where there is vibration/movement. The first level is you moving into the astral/psychic fourth dimension, reflecting the disembodied third dimension you presently live in. This first level contains all your dreams, nightmares, emotions and thoughts. You move on to where there is no time or distance, experiencing many disconnected experiences from your past. Gradually all of this moves from a denser light to a lighter light. You are in a higher frequency/realm of existence. You now meet your spirit guide who takes your hand, as you see everything around you shifting into harmony and balance and beauty. You feel a joy you have never felt before and know this is where the world is headed.

These records are a blueprint/template to the new world paradigm of unity and Oneness. As you absorb all the beauty around you, you realize your guide has taken you to the Hall of Records. It is a crystal, high hall temple with no walls nor ceiling; stored within the crystals are all the records of everything. You then come upon a cosmic angel librarian looking very much like the old white bearded pictures of God you saw as a child. This cosmic being hands you a beautiful crystal that contains a complete record of all your lives -- all the lessons you have learned and still need to learn. In an instant, you experience and integrate the wisdom that lives within the crystal. Now you need to maintain and sustain that wisdom as you return to your dense carbon based physical body. **This is the mission of all your lives.**

Beloved humans, you can create your own passageway to The Akashic Records (accessing information at higher frequencies of awareness/consciousness) or use the above symbolic example anytime you wish simply by asking to be taken there. Once you retrieve a record, how you choose to apply it is within your freedom of choice and will. Since The Akashic Records contain everything, the information most often given is what you need to know or would most support you in that exact moment. Each time you come back into The Akashic Records you will receive additional insights.

Each of you has been creating your reality through your emotions and thoughts, past, present and future. All of these times are really the now; the past was once the now. The present is the now, and the future will become the now. You can think of The Akashic Records segmented into these three time zones -- past, present and future. Since The Akashic Records live within the now, you can see into your (the) past, present and future, and glean life reviews and previews that serve your highest good, and what is needed to fully activate your soul plan, your reason to be here through your talents and gifts by knowing who you are and why you are here.

Medical intuitives, psychic (disembodied third

dimensional) fourth dimensional connections, karma (past life memory) and higher realms fifth dimensional teachings are some lesser and greater examples of what can be accessed through The Akashic Records. Karma is a past life memory in the present containing positive and negative resolved and unresolved issues. You pick up all relationships good and bad exactly where you left them off. This way you learn what you need to learn when you need to learn it.

The Akashic Records are filled with unlimited teaching tools from positive and negative habits, rituals and patterns from the past that can be re-activated by your emotions and thoughts, thus actions in the present. Some of your 'comfort zones' relate to positive talents and gifts while others reflect negative ones. Each of these is basically the manifestation of what your soul plan chooses to integrate with its previous choices/experiences. You can choose to be a healer from a previous life experience or continue to act out sociopathic behavior from the past. You will continue these behaviors until you have learned what you need to learn.

Following the Universal Laws of Attraction, The Akashic Records bring forth the people who mirror your own strengths and weaknesses. When you experience something you like or dislike in another, it is something you need to address within yourself. No matter how it feels, each experience has the potential to be supportive and loving in regard to the activation/growth/expansion of your soul plan (your reason to be here). This planet is a 'Lover-versity' of learning how to love self, thus others. In effect, Mother Earth is a classroom of cause and effect where you routinely have the opportunity to meet self and apply universal/spiritual truths within your three dimensional world.

Your ultimate mission is to increase your vibration/frequency in order to transcend the third dimension. Your success with lessons learned, or not, determines the next pathway of experiences that your soul plan attracts to it. When you have had enough of negative consequences you will begin to make other choices (responsibility=consequence). Your freedom of choice and will is tied tightly to how well you interface with the lessons The Akashic Records brings forth.

Since The Akashic Records reside within the now they employ an eternal library of possibilities and probabilities. The now containing the past and the present is not constant and shifts with every emotion and thought you have, every choice you make through your freedom of choice and will. Remember the past and the future are dependent upon what you do in the present and what you choose to learn in the past and the future. You are continuously 'receiving' wisdom from The Akashic Records, often through your intuition and dreams. What you do with this information is up to you.

It is essential that you know at this time that The Akashic Records are in service and responsible for attracting to each soul exactly what he or she needs. The Akashic Records and your Divine Soul Plan are constantly calculating all your possible choices through your free will. When you enter the fourth dimension, the psychic/astral realm, during sleep, you often tune into your possible future through dreams or during the day in a deja vu moment. In effect, both of these experiences are connecting into a higher frequency of consciousness (a mini-Ascension Process).

The Akashic Records are so much more than a magical memory database. They are interactive with the present affecting the revealing, integrating with the future. Moment to moment you are continuously interfacing with The Akashic Records uploading experiences you need that serve your highest good and that of others. The Akashic Records are your personal processing 'workshop' for accessing lessons learned and the ones still needed to achieve self-mastery and full activation of your soul plan (your reason to be here). **Please accept with compassion and forgive that each of you is exactly where you are for a divine reason. All your incarnational cycles are proceeding as divinely planned. There is no need to compare yourself to anyone else.**

Your modern sciences are beginning to catch up to how something like The Akashic Records actually exists or works. Science, energy and spirit are finally merging, which is your destiny. This merger will set you free from much of your lack, limitation and duality of the past and present. Your science of quantum physics shows there are active electro-magnetic frequencies that also exist within informational frequencies. These allow motion without regard for time or distance or simultaneous telepathic transmission of information regardless of time or distance. These frequencies contain consciousness and what you would call intelligence and are the guidance system for the constant expansion of creation. It is your destiny to soon tap into these electro-magnetic frequencies within and surrounding your planet for free fuel for all. This will shift your current governmental, political and economic systems towards We Consciousness/Unity Consciousness. (This channel has written in detail on the electro-magnetic grid. This information is available to you simply by asking).

DIVINE DISCUSSIONS

Whether you choose to view The Akashic Records from a spiritual/energetic point of view or an existing scientific perspective, the fact that they exist (the purpose of this message) demonstrates there is a loving Creator who intends to assist you in waking up to your True Divine Nature by your knowing and applying the reason for your existence: **To Learn To Love And Be In Service To One Another And The World.**

Your inquiring human minds might continue to ask, "Where is all this going to lead?" Your souls are destined to eternally grow and expand as you, being the Creator, continue as master teachers assisting in the creation of communities and worlds of equality, harmony and balance throughout this solar system, galaxy, universe and multiverse. You and Creation become One, as it is written within The Akashic Records.

Adama's Message

From: Adama, The Father of Humanity, High Priest of Telos, Lemuria, Inner Earth Civilization, speaking of two previous journeys to Mt. Shasta.

Greetings,

Your father is coming to you at this time, your father of Lemuria, known to you as Adama.

Dear ones, as you wander through your wandering, we are here in remembrance of the journeys we did together, the journeys that your beloved Archangel Michael, in combination with we of the Lemurian Gateways, took to join above and below energies.

We ask you at this time to review the rituals performed during the past two sacred journeys (see *Coming Home To Lemuria, An Ascension Adventure Story*) that activated portals and vortices throughout the central vortex of our ancient native home, Mt. Shasta, to radiate out through the entire planet.

You will begin to see, as you review the rituals within your journey number one, the pattern of what is happening in the rest of your world. Within those rituals is the formula for your Ascension Process. Within those rituals is the information that you will continue to receive from other frequencies -- Archangelic, Inner Earth, Inter- Galactic and Star Fields as well, dear ones.

We ask you, further, to reconnect with the significance of why you chose and were chosen to be proxies for humanity. What you are clearing and cleansing within yourselves individually, in your personal process, is a reflection of what is taking place in the macro/micro relationship with the planet, both within and upon her body, dear ones.

You have chosen and picked up, if you will, the continued mission and journey from previous lifetimes, which emanate and commence within the Lemurian culture, segueing into the Atlantean culture, segueing into the creation of Egypt, Aztec and the Mayan civilizations and others as well, dear ones, which will be revealed to you in specific geographic locations upon the face of the planet.

As humanity continues clearing and cleansing the aspects that reflect the Ascension Process of our home, Mother Gaia, much will be revealed within you. We continue to work in concert with the Archangelic Realms, specifically Archangel Michael, who is an essential aspect of this band of consciousness, this frequency, to create what became of this planet and humanity itself.

The beginnings and the origin of your species (see previous article "A New Creation Story" on page 4) have been hidden from humanity. The aspects of humanity that are clearing and cleansing at this time are a reflection of your origins, which you are preparing yourselves to believe and to know as the truth of humanity's creation. Within that, the aspect of Divinity was never lost, which you are in the process of reconnecting with at this time, dear ones.

Know that your individual, individuated soul plan journeys are a reflection and a mirroring of the planet herself, dear ones. And we ask you to remember the agreement that you signed on to before coming here and being a part of this process through learning what is through what is not.

You are involved in the end game, the end timeline of duality, separation and confrontation. That is why planet Earth appears to be in such upheaval at this time. You are actually reaching an apex of disruption in order to begin following the other line of that apex. That line, that journey, is to your Divinity.

You are very near to connecting and being able to assimilate the union of our civilizations, Inner and Outer Earth. Once that takes place the entire mysteries and wisdoms of the universe and creation will be revealed, for you will be ready, as you would say, to handle it. At this time, you are not.

Again, please know the connection between the journeys that you chose and were chosen for. We ask you to review those in combination with your individual soul plans in combination with that of the planet. This is no small task that you signed up for.

For the channel that we are coming through now, the reason we asked that all of those rituals and pieces of information be put into an easily attained format (see *Coming Home To Lemuria, An Ascension Adventure Story*) was so those who choose and resonate with reviewing that information will also become proxies for humanity and will ratchet out and ratchet out and ratchet out.

You will soon find others to be in partnership with that. They will join you on your journey and the spreading of your soul plans, of your mission, of your reason to be here.

Love, dear ones, love one another. It has been taught

and taught and taught. Are you ready through the Christ Consciousness energy coming through you and to you, by being this energy itself, to embrace brotherhood and the love of one another and free yourselves of the way you have chosen to learn through your wounds, defenses, separations, your what is not, to move fully, lovingly into what is?

We will connect with you again soon, as well as with Archangel Michael and other wisdoms, to empower, lead, guide, and to love you.

Akhenaten/Moses And Me

From: Akhenaten/Moses and the Great White Brotherhood.

We of the Great White Brotherhood, in conjunction with the Akhenaten/Moses energy, come to you at this time within your evolutionary process of Ascension with more truth of your past and how that is affecting your present. It is your Divine Destiny to know the truth.

Beloveds, the meaning, value and purpose of the Great White Brotherhood is Self-Empowerment within the dimension you presently reside. As with the channel with who we are coming through now, our intention is to open each divine soul to direct contact with their God Power/Source energy. This will leave no one dependent upon others, but, rather, empowered in their own soul plan/life with true connection to truth. There is much deceit and denial of deceit within your world. It is your destiny for this to end. True power is never power over another. It is standing within your own God Power for the good of all with grace and ease.

Many of the teachings/wisdoms within The Angel News Network and many other endeavors are about bringing the tools of Life/Self Mastery to you at this time to free you from yourselves. Are you ready to receive these tools?

Your lives were never meant to be the struggle they are. If you so choose, it is time to choose self-empowerment over victimhood and the control of others. Through ownership of how you have chosen to learn, it is time to make other choices. These words represent the tenets and codes of the Great White Brotherhood.

The Great White Brotherhood consists of higher realm beings of unlimited power who disseminate spiritual teachings to humans whose soul plans include receiving these wisdoms: becoming Masters of the Ancient Wisdoms or the Ascended Masters. So in effect, we of the Great White Brotherhood are enlightened beings guiding the spiritual development of the human race. We are also known as Great Brotherhood of Light or the Spiritual Hierarchy of Earth. The name *brotherhood* includes the balance of the masculine and feminine energies, and the term *white* refers to white light as opposed to darkness. Here are a few of our members who you may know: Master Jesus/Lord Sananda, Mother Mary, Gautama Buddha, Saint Germaine, Hilarion, Kuthumi, Confucius, Kwan Yin, Archangel Michael and Uriel. All of these beings and more are here to assist whatever needs healing to advance the spiritual well-being of humanity. Simply ask and you will receive.

Akhenaten/Moses

It is time, dear ones, to connect we of the Great White Brotherhood with a being who brought great light into your world and laid the foundation for many of your spiritual/religious endeavors and wisdoms (even though they have often been corrupted by humanity). This individual is the Egyptian pharaoh Akhenaten and the Biblical Moses *who are one and the same*. The name Moses means 'heir' or 'born of.' Thus, Moses is a title rather than a name. This truth will put a new spin on your religious and spiritual history and how you think about yourselves and your present world. **The reason we are coming through this channel at this time is that he and a *soul brother* shared the incarnation of the way shower, Akhenaten/Moses.** One individual allowed the maturation of Akhenaten/Moses; the other brought in the Great White Brotherhood energies when needed. These two served as proxies for humanity.

We bring in the present incarnational cycles information to show you as a human species you are in the process of clearing and cleansing past lives that are affecting the present. You are all in the process of healing past and present lives, passed on from generation to generation, to set yourselves free from their wounds and defenses in order to move into a higher frequency of existence/consciousness. This is affecting personal and world events since they are all connected.

Dear ones, through your freedom of choice and will and your discernment, you will decide what is true for you (what you apply or not) as we continue. Many other sources at present are also bringing this truth to you. Recently discovered ancient documents such as the Sumerian cuneiform tablets (your first form of writing after the last fall from Truth), the Dead Sea Scrolls and Emerald Tablets support the premise: *there is much correction needed in your view of history*. You do not yet have a true view of your history and exactly where you are headed. This new applied knowledge (wisdom) will assist in freeing you from yourselves, religions, governments and corporations. Soon you will have a new worldview of your history that will support a shift in awareness.

Akhenaten/Moses Speaks

To those meant to hear me, I, Akhenaten was born in Year 12 of my father Amenhotep III, 1,394 BC, in our lovely summer royal palace in now what is called northern Sinai (where there is currently so much unrest). This is the same location where Moses was born according to your history. Many of you know *the baby-in-the-bulrushes story.* It all had to do with my mother's bloodline not being good enough for me to be king.

During my early years, mother kept me, Akhenaten/Moses, away from royal residences so I would not be killed. Later I was moved to Heliopolis, north of Cairo, to receive my initiations/education under the supervision of Anen the priest of Ra, the prevailing religion at the time. When I was sixteen, I was allowed to appear at the capital of Thebes. It was here I met my half-sister Nefertiti for the first time. My non-handsome self fell in love with her beauty on first sight. We were two lost souls meant to join in a twin flame and shift human history forever. As Nefertiti was the heiress to the throne, our relationship was encouraged since it strengthened my right to follow father on the throne.

Following my marriage to Nefertiti, I was appointed (by Amenhotep III) to an important political/religious position, which upset the prevailing priests of Amun (the controlling religion at the time) and reactivated a long time dispute. On my accession to the throne, I took the name of Amenhotep IV. My beloved Nefertiti strongly supported me and took a prominent position in all official occasions and on all monuments during the early years of my reign. The conflict and hostility that surrounded me at the time of my birth resurfaced.

When the Amun priest objected even more to my power, I responded by building various temples at Karnak and Memphis to our new God, Aten (the concept/truth of one Supreme Being). I was not a good politician and ignored the old priests and often banned them from festivities. I eventually only allowed our one-god Aten by changing my name to AkhenATEN in honor of our new deity, Aten. The raging Egyptian establishment viewed Aten as a challenger who would replace the powerful state god Amun and would not be under Amun's control. You are presently freeing yourselves from such control.

These were tense days. Eventually I was persuaded to reach a compromise by establishing a new capital in Middle Egypt, at Amama on the east bank of the Nile, some two hundred miles north of Thebes. The situation did calm down following my departure to Thebes, as I ruled alone. We built a beautiful city, Akhenaten, the Horizon of Aten, parallel to the Nile, and we were free to worship our God. Today, dear ones, you can still see what remains of this glorious time and my Nefertiti depicted as having equal stature with the king (balance of the masculine and feminine energies).

Aten was depicted by a disc at the top of royal scenes, extending its rays towards the king and queen, with the rays ending in our hands holding the Ankh, the Egyptian cross symbol of eternal life. **Through receiving the Great White Brotherhood energies, I conceived (re-introduced) a single controlling intelligence above and below all beings, including the human gods.**

Akhenaten's Reign

During my reign, with the ascended master's support of the Great White Brotherhood, I was able to abolish the complex pantheon of the ancient Egyptian religion and replace it with a single God concept, Aten, who was unseen. This is the same soul plan/purpose as the one you call Moses, and the basis for much of your spiritual/religious knowledge today.

In review of my Moses/Akhenaten's incarnation: I was

brought up by Israelite relatives, ruled Egypt for seventeen years and angered many of my subjects by replacing the traditional Egyptian gods with the one god, Aten. I was led to re-introduce **monotheism** to this world and then was forced to eventually abdicate the throne, retreating to exile in Sinai with my Egyptian and Israelite supporters. I died at the hands of Seti I while attempting to regain power. *I did all this to impregnate this planet with the Christ Consciousness Oneness energies of the Great White Brotherhood of which this channel and his soul brother (the one now called Omar -- meaning, he that speaks, living a long life) were joined as me -- Akhenaten. It is time to speak again the truth and allow it to integrate into our eternal lives: to heal the past into the present.*

In Conclusion

The remaining and resounding truth of my life is that we are all one; the one who may appear your oppressor is your salvation. When I received The Ten Commandments there was no official Hebrew language at the time. *The Egyptian Book of the Dead* and *The Ten Commandments* are the same messages. Rosicrucians, founded upon Great White Brotherhood wisdom, have been teaching all of which we speak for centuries. It just may be time to rewrite the Old Testament Christian and Hebrew Bibles, the *Talmud*, Jewish *Cabala*, the *Koran*, Arab history and release the hidden ancient documents within the Vatican vaults in order to allow you to know the truth. Much of your duality and confrontation today is based upon you not knowing you are each other. It is time for this separation to end, if you so choose. You are your brother's keeper. There is plenty for all; simply ask each what you need and how you are feeling. Dear ones, you are each other in disguise. It is time to drop the veil and see you are all one experiencing one another, including God. This message/teaching was/is the soul plan (political and religious activist) of my incarnation as Akhenaten/Moses. If you so choose, now apply the truth spoken once again into your present lives and world and manifest the creation of a world of equality, harmony and balance which I began so many centuries ago...

There Is Only One.

DIVINE DISCUSSIONS

Archangels Gabriel And Raphael

Interview with Archangels Gabriel and Raphael, Featuring Channel Phillip Elton Collins and Spiritual Journalist Joel Anastasi.

Note: This interview occurred after releasing the "Sacred Trilogy Of Teachings," which includes the "Seven Sacred Flames," "Sacred Shifts To Ascend" and "Seven Sacred Steps," and in preparation for a *Divine Discussions* gathering.

Greetings Beloveds,

Beloved humans being human upon the surface of this planet, we greet you. These are the combined energies of Archangel Gabriel and Raphael.

We come to you at this time to review and prepare you for your final gathering in regard to **the meaning of life, the true cause and cure of disease** in your 3D frequency.

1. First, briefly review the "Sacred Trilogy Of Teachings" (pages 167-192).

2. Then move into the final aspect of this teaching, which are the energetic exercises (see PhillipEltonCollins.com/event/july-9-2015-divine-discussions).

The meaning, value and purpose of these exercises are to release the energetic blockages, the armoring around yourselves, from past and present incarnational cycles, in order to regain the balance of energy in your body, which facilitates true and permanent healing.

ALPHABETICAL LISTING OF ARTICLES: A

Angels: The awakening of the soul is an aspect of the healing. Through the actual healing process itself, you are reconnecting and awakening with the fragments of the soul plan. That awakening facilitates true and permanent healing. Use your own resonance and discernment whether you think this will add clarity or confusion, dear one.

Trust that you have within you through your internal resonance and internal gyro system what you need to go forward. Trust, relax and surrender and you will be guided.

Joel: The teaching is about health and healing. Can you offer any counsel for the channel who has been experiencing so many health challenges?

Angels: The channel is aware that what he is physically experiencing is the result of *releasing, clearing and cleansing his physical format from past and present lives* to allow this divine soul who chose, and has been chosen, *to be a channel for these particular frequencies to be an even clearer channel.* It is a matter of releasing from physical cellular memory, stored emotions and thoughts in order to become clearer.

Joel: Phillip is one of the clearest channels I have encountered, so it will be interesting to see what kind of additional clarity he will achieve.

Angels: The channel is reaching exponentially farther and farther out into higher and higher realms of resonance and connection -- moving from earth and this particular solar system into galactic, universal, and even multi-versal frequencies. This channel integrates the macro and micro wisdoms within these frequencies, without overloading humanity with information it might not be ready for at this time but giving a micro/macro perspective as a key component of this individual's Divine Soul Plan.

Joel: Phillip and I have a natural ability to work together. Can you offer any observations about our pairing of gifts and talents?

Angels: It is an essential aspect of your soul plan. It is the core issue of your soul plans to be doing and being what you are presently doing and being. Whenever you evaluate something through grace and ease, it is an indication that you are on the right track.

It is important to the soul we are coming through at this time. He understands it is his responsibility to make himself available.

Joel: Phillip is much more available than I have found other channels to be.

Angels: This channel understands the essential responsibility of that and most often does not allow his wounds and defenses to get in the way of that responsibility and choice and through that choice being chosen for this work. It is his core reason for remaining here.

Joel: Our recent work with the Francis energy gave us a chance to get a spiritual perspective on Earth events. I thought that was a good mission to incorporate in The Angel News Network (ANN) and *Divine Discussions*.

Angels: Not everyone will relate to it. It is a matter of resonance. A core issue of humanity at this time, and the responsibilities of the Archangelic Realms, is the relationship that humanity is having with itself and how this is ratcheting out in its relationship to others on the planet. Many of these unhealed or shut down aspects are the result of the origin of the species of this planet, having the wisdom of how that origin began, and how it is affecting current events.

Tying in what the higher realms have to say about current events is an aspect of the Whole (of *All That Is*) and not the whole (of planet Earth). The core issue again is the relationship with self; *Archangel Michael*, most importantly, and *Uriel*, as well as *Raphael* and we of *Gabriel* are coming together to really mirror your relationship with yourselves and how that is affecting the rest of your world. For, in effect, you are Creation. You are the Universe reflecting itself out to the world and the universe. It is a mirror of self.

So within your human contract you have chosen to experience what is through what is not (through duality/separation, often leading to confrontations). You are now experiencing exacerbations of this behavior, which appear to be the worst it has ever been. In reality, it is not. All of this is needing to come up through the Ascension Process to heal--within the channel, within the planet it is coming up for review at this time. It is all in *Divine Order* no matter how things look from the outside.

Joel: Adama and St. Germaine say they continue to knock on my door during the Ascension Chair ceremony. Can you offer suggestions for how I can respond to the knocking of spirit?

Angels: As the divine soul you call the channel began,

mark your calendar for a 50-day period becoming aware each day that higher realms are knocking. It is a combination of you choosing as an aspect of your soul plan, or not; if you say yes, then being chosen to be a channel of these particular frequencies. There is no right or wrong in this, dear one, no good or bad within it. Whatever decision you make will be in perfect *Divine Order*. It is the destiny of humanity to become multi-dimensional and to be connected to these higher realms. It is your destiny to be connected to the higher realms.

You have channeled in many past lives when you were an aspect of particular golden ages past, be they Lemurian, Atlantis, early Egypt, Greece, Aztec, Mayan, Hopi or many other past golden ages. So you will decide using your freedom of choice and will within the next 50-day period and make your choice. See these 50 days as a preparation for healing and releasing any resistance, any wounding or defense, which has impeded this process in the past.

Joel: Which energy am I being chosen for?

Angels: We are inviting you to open yourself to the Gabriel energy.

Joel: What about the Mary energy?

Angels: What does your resonance say?

Joel: Both.

Angels: Then so be it dear one. It is your choice. Remember, the first ingredient is you choosing. Sometimes you're conscious of it. Sometimes you're not. When the Uriel energy was knocking on the door of this channel, he was completely unaware of it as were many colleagues of your past.

Joel: Some of my readings include Tom Kenyon and Ruth Montgomery, but Ruth's prophecies were largely wrong. How trustworthy are her books as a grounding for spiritual understanding?

Angels: The 5D Energies do not deal with prophecy. They do not predict the future. That frequency is astral, psychic, what you call 4D -- a disembodied reflection of 3D where you reside at this time. What you were experiencing with this particular individual was her ability to connect with the astral, the psychic, the 4D and bring what she received through her filter out into the world. It is not our responsibility or our desire to predict or to prophesize the future. That would interfere with your freedom of choice and will. We have no way or desire to interfere with your freedom of choice and of will.

This channel has a powerful psychic ability. He chose and made a decision to not work in that frequency even though he had a tremendous gift within it. And to move beyond it is an aspect of his soul plan. That was the knock, knock, knocking of the initial Uriel energy. If you read and study the material coming through this channel, you will see it is not about prophecy.

Joel: Sure, I transcribed a lot of it. I'm well aware of that.

Angels: It's about bringing messages and tools to your frequency in order to set you free from it, to release yourself from it, which is your Divine Destiny.

Joel: Bringing messages and tools is also how I see Tom Kenyon's work. I'd be very interested in hearing your perspective on the value of his work and also about the spiritual salon gatherings (small gatherings of people in a home) I am facilitating. I'm planning to show a film on Tom's work at the next salon.

Angels: You are following your resonance and discernment, where other messengers are bringing messages and tools to humanity--in preparation to do the same yourself, if you so choose, dear one. You have heard this before. So you have an exercise now, a 50-day process and be aware what the 50th day will be when you figure that out on your calendar. You are following examples, such as the channel you are connecting with at this time and other Divine Soul Plans, as a preamble and an example of who you could become and how you could become it, if you so choose. Does that resonate?

Joel: It does. Phillip and I re-met 20 years ago this coming Labor Day weekend. It was a low point for both of us at that time. The meeting on a beach in Fire Island kind of changed the course of both of our lives. We seem to have such a powerful connection, if not always enjoying each other, LOL. We seem to have a destiny of working together and empowering each other to contributing to spiritual life here on earth. What would you say about this powerful connection that is now almost 40 years old since we first met?

Angels: Yes, look at the synchronicity of those connections. And it is the synchronicity of how it began and where it is at present, which is a pathway to the activation of your individual and collective soul plans.

Follow the resonance, discernment and feelings that you have about the work that is transpiring by being together and the work that you are doing now. These are, if you so choose, the higher reasons for your synchronicity.

Joel: Yes, you're just confirming the truth of what I believe.

Angels: The truth is gained through your resonance and discernment and the emotion that you feel around it.

Joel: How might the channel strengthen himself physically?

Angels: The channel is in a process of clearing what needs to be cleared and cleansed. He is very aware of what needs to takes place physically and is taking care of that.

Joel: Does the channel's filter influence anything coming from you that the channel should be aware of?

Angels: Every channel has a filter that reflects aspects and components of their soul plan, components of themselves that need to heal and be released. The channel is aware that he has had many powerful incarnational cycles in the past. There has been abuse of power, a struggle of love versus power within these incarnational cycles. Even within this recent incarnational cycle, the channel was given many opportunities to walk through the abuse of power and has consciously decided not to do that. That does not mean that the abuses of power in the past do not still reside in the cellular memory of this individual. He has chosen this lifetime through the illnesses that he has experienced, to clear and cleanse those as much as possible in this incarnational cycle to continue his destiny and the activation of his soul plan.

Joel: I am trying to create a new life here. Can you offer any guidance on creating a healthy balance of giving and receiving? That has been difficult, and I don't know if I'm barking up the wrong tree or if there is a potential for a loving, rewarding relationship. Any observations about the potential to achieve that?

Angels: It is all what you choose through your freedom of choice and freedom of will. In each and every relationship there is the possibility of a loving relationship. There is the possibility of loving and supporting one another that is always possible. Look at the areas where duality has created your separation and at this juncture in your life, ask yourself, what do I need? What would I like to have within my life as a co-creator of my life? Is there something within individuals that I am resisting in receiving?

You have, through relationships, brought up many negative and positive aspects and still survived at some point. When the relationship is working on a higher realm, which allows the maintaining and sustaining of it, or within the 3D element, you have certainly thrust wounds and defenses at one another aplenty, have you not?

The fact that you are able to surrender to the higher realm aspects of what you have to offer one another is simply up to you. You are entering an eighth decade within this incarnational cycle. Simply ask yourself, what do I need? What resonates for me? What discerns for me? In my loneliness, am I being careful not to bring others in simply to prevent myself from being lonely and allow myself to be with myself in a loving, supportive relationship without being lonely, being alone without being lonely?

Evaluate whether bringing in an individual more permanently into your life is a fix to that or is truly a love force, a committed love force that you wish to have within your life. The channel has found a partner who brings peace, joy, simplicity, a quietness and lack of drama into his life that is needed in order for him to complete his soul plan as a channel and messenger of these higher realms. Ask yourself, would being connected to an individual facilitate that? Does that help you?

Joel: You nailed it exactly -- peace, joy, quiet, lack of drama. That is what I want. I guess what I hunger for mostly is community as well as a personal relationship.

Angels: You live in an aspect of a geography where creating community is a bit of a challenge because of the relationship with self that many are having. Be aware of that. It makes the work that you and the channel do even more essential of bringing that light into this particular vortex. It is a density that has been created largely upon duality and separation.

You're very close to the residue of the Atlantean energy. Based upon that frequency, that density of energy, corrupted energy, if you will, that attracted many individuals to this aspect of the world to escape, to hide, to be in separation and duality. It explains a lot of your patterns of behavior in this culture in this particular location.

Joel: Can you offer suggestions to make the salons a rich, supportive environment?

Angels: Be and do it for yourself. Give to yourself what you wish to give to others.

Joel: Interesting. That is what I'm doing with the Tom Kenyon work. I see its value and I'll be sharing it with others in the next salon.

Angels: The channel has a karmic connection to not only yourself but to your other brethren in the endeavor you call The Angel News Network. He is a guardian, a godfather, a protectorate, and in many ways that spills over in your relationship as well. Are you aware of that?

Joel: I see that more between Phillip and Jeff. Not that Phillip hasn't been loving and protective with me. I see Phillip and I as having more of an even relationship in terms of the qualities we bring to each other.

Angels: Well you have your chronology, and you have had many of the same world experiences that allow a connection. That does not necessarily exist with the other brethren.

Joel: Can you give me more information about our past karmic connection?

Angels: In this incarnational cycle, many of you have come together again for a continuation, and in some ways, a completion of what has started in the past. You have had a connection with this divine soul in Atlantis, Egypt, and in Lemuria. There have been times when you have set upon a path of contribution to your civilizations and that became interrupted for various reasons. This is a continuation of that pattern. Does that help you?

Joel: Yes, but it makes me hungry for more information.

Angels: And what would you do with that information?

Joel: I probably shouldn't need any more information because you have made it very clear that it's about intentions and fulfilling what I am moved to do and be in my life, which doesn't depend very much on that kind of information.

Angels: You have heard the expression, 'The Grand Reunion,' which the channel has said many times. It is a grand reunion of all of you who are together who are resonating with one another or you wouldn't be gathering in the same resonance.

Joel: I have been exposed to so many tantalizing little bits of information from Adama and others that alluded to Phillip coming on the original ship that came to Earth and things like that. You can't hear things like that as a human being without wondering, Wow, that sounds very Star Wars and wondering, what was my role in all of that and what was my connection, all that kind of stuff.

Angels: You were connected throughout those incarnational cycles. There are details of information, which may or may not help you at this time, if you can accept with compassion and forgive, and assimilate, that you have had repeated connections. Any of you who have resonance and discernment with one another sees that feeling of resonance and discernment as a pathway of continuation of something from the past or it wouldn't be there. And you can go into the details of that. Going through past life regression often can prevent the experience of the present.

Joel: I am going to engage the 50-day exercise you suggested. Anything more you would say about that? That is pretty important. This could be the beginning of the next step that I take. I find that exciting.

Angels: If you so choose, dear one.

Joel: I do choose. You know already I choose. This isn't a surprise. What else is my life about?

Angels: Well, let's talk about what happens within that 50-day process. That is what your mental body is hungering for. As we said, it is an opportunity to begin to release and heal in a wounded defense or resistance that which lies within you that has been preventing it in the past by setting an actual time line. It gives you an opportunity to know that, yes a potential process is in progress. It allows you to become conscious of that process on a calibrated, constant basis, in this case 50 days. And it allows you to make a decision at the end of it, which in many ways that decision has already been made on some levels. But it just gives you an opportunity to begin to trust and surrender, see yourself good enough to be the communicator that you are saying you are choosing to be.

Joel: We have had a wonderful, rich conversation. Thanks so much for coming to us. Anything you want to add?

Angels: We will resume on your *Divine Discussions* gathering later in your week. We will review what we brought out to humanity, which will be repeated and repeated and repeated, in this teaching of what is life, and what is the cause and effect and true cure of disease? That is an ongoing process within humanity, and we will present together the energetic exercises, which very powerfully begin to break the armoring and the imbalances that exist within your physical format. We shall resume and connect at a later moment.

Joel: Thank you so much.

At Present

From: Ascended Master Energies.

Dear Beloved Human Beings,

We who once walked upon the surface of this planet, like you do now (and have chosen to ascend to a higher frequency existence which is your destiny also), come to you at this crucial time within your evolutionary process. We have neither intention nor ability to interfere with your freedom of choice or will but come to you with a higher perspective view. From our advantage point, you can choose to make new decisions or not. Much of what you are experiencing has to do with the origin of the human species on this planet and the healing process that is taking place at this time. Many of your higher aspects have been shut down in order to attempt to maintain control, but this is shifting at present.

If you so choose it is time to wake up and become aware of the ancient hidden forces (with no national, political, or religious boundaries) attempting to control what they did not create on this planet. This attempted control for eons has kept you in duality, separation and confrontation. Their game plan is to create chaos from events they create in order to keep you from knowing the truth of their existence. Often times these hidden forces are within your present governmental and leadership roles. Please remember, dear fellow humans, you ultimately **cannot control what you did not create.** *This cosmic law will allow you to escape and move beyond the events you are currently creating.* If you so choose, accept and know the truth of what we have repeatedly brought you through the ages.

Since your planet is experiencing the final cycle of its Ascension Process of moving from a carbon based, dualistic existence, returning to the Love and Light from whence we all came, we are receiving dispensations from galactic and universal forces to further assist you. If it resonates from your sacred hearts, call upon us to guide and support you.

Remember, dear humans, you have chosen to learn the way you are learning, and you can make other choices at this time **by knowing the truth will set you free**. Through the *consequences of your learning process*, you are creating unified fields of love and support for one another: learning what is through what is not.

Know You Are Loved and Supported.

Alphabetical Listing Of Articles: B

Being A Channel Of Higher Realms
Being Co-Creator: From Child To Adult
Being Human

Being A Channel Of Higher Realms

From: Phillip Elton Collins.

We are all designed and destined to be channels of higher realms, communicating with frequencies and consciousness beyond the human mind and bringing that wisdom into humanity. In fact, it has never not been that way. All of our past golden ages, be they Lemurian, Atlantean, Egyptian, Greek, Aztec, Mayan or otherwise, were supported and created by higher realms, support beyond the human experience. Entertain the thought that the human mind is a receiver of these higher wisdoms. We have never been alone. In the past, this was common knowledge. It is time for this to be common again.

Many people ask me, "**How can I become a channel of higher realms?**" having experienced my classes where individuals interact with these higher realms themselves or having read one of my several books filled with teachings and tools from various high frequency sources (Archangelic Realms, Ascended Masters, Inter-Galactic, Inner Earth Civilizations, Nature Spirits, etc.). My books (*sent from higher realms*) are in a variety of formats -- from true adventure stories, to sacred poetry, phrases of presence, teachings and tools that cover where we came from and why we are here, personal process exercises to assist in healing our wounds and ego defenses and even a divine dictionary of metaphysical terms (all these channeled and not from my mind). At this point, there are hundreds of topics I have received that expand the truth and wisdom of being human. **My response to how** to become a channel often is, how can you not channel, since *being a channel is nothing special, an essential aspect of being human?* Run the other way if anyone tells you otherwise! There can be *no worshipping the guru* in higher realm channeling, and most importantly, you need to *use your own resonance and discernment* with any information that comes through anyone. If it does not feel or sound right to you, do not apply it. If it does, go for it.

Realizing there is wisdom more expansive and wiser than the human mind or experience is a challenge for many. Often times our *educated intelligence* gets in the way. But someday, soon, it will return to being not a big deal and a common occurrence (it already is for many of us). In the meantime, I shall share some of my experiences of being a channel and see if it helps you in any way to be and do the same. For those of you already channeling, please allow this to be a further affirmation of the great gift you are bringing to our world in assisting our advancement as a human species.

In my being a higher realm channel, I never attempt to convince or prove to others this is real. That would be *trying to control* them. I have no desire to do that. I simply say, if the message resonates, apply it. If it does not, throw it out the proverbial window.

For me, being a channel is a *joyful experience* of choosing and being chosen to connect with various frequencies (an aspect of my Divine Soul Plan) and being able to bring their truth and teaching into our world.

One of the fun ways of doing this, at present, is with my colleague Joel Anastasi. We have a **radio show** where I go into trance and **Joel interviews these realms about current events from a higher realm perspective.** It always fascinates me how these realms take the drama out of things and reveal the true cause and effect of events in our life and world.

There are basically **two types of fifth dimensional channels; trance and conscious.** Trance channels are completely taken over by the frequency and do not know what is happening. Conscious channels are partially awake and have some idea of what is going on. I am a conscious channel. **Channels of fifth dimensional frequencies are not psychic nor astral mediums.** We do not predict the future or tell you what to do; that is fourth dimensional (psychic/astral) mediumship. The fourth dimension, without time or distance, is a disembodied reflection of the third dimension where we reside now. **The fifth dimensional frequencies with which I connect (Archangelic Realms, Ascended Masters, Inter-Galactic, Inner Earth and Nature Spirits) present universal and cosmic wisdoms that allow the individual to choose for themselves which path to take through their freedom of choice and will: Maintaining and sustaining a process of inside out, not outside in.** Fifth dimensional frequencies are two levels higher than third-dimensional (the human experience) and one level higher than the psychic/astral fourth dimension. Higher does not mean better; it simply means it is higher in vibration and has access to universal wisdoms.

There are aspects of humanity that are more and more beginning to accept the contribution of wisdom that comes through fifth dimensional channeling. Let me give another personal example, and see if it supports your desire to channel. There is a well-known **cultural** museum, owned by a large private university, which had a marvelous pre-Inca exhibition. This pre-Inca civilization had no written language, and the scientist and educators could not figure out how they had developed such an advanced culture with so many surviving fascinating artifacts. I suggested to one of the directors at the museum, who also taught postgraduate programs at the university, let us recreate the ancient temple and allow me to go into trance and connect with the remaining consciousness of that civilization to allow them to explain who they were and how they achieved what they did.

Once in trance, within the reformation of an ancient temple complex, complete with music from ancient instruments, I connected with a priest from this past advanced culture who explained they were telepathic, thus the reason for no written language, and that they were connected to higher realms who taught them the needed technology to achieve what they did. The channeling lasted over an hour, answering many questions and concerns of this past world. Then we opened to questions and answers to the scientific and educational audience. What people would accept was up to them.

I was in service to being the messenger of this wisdom, and it mattered not to me who believed what was presented. **For many in the audience this was a completely new precedent to learn beyond the human mind within a museum owned by a university.**

Another way I am in service to being a messenger of these higher realm frequencies is that my Angel News Network colleagues, trance channel Jeff Fasano and spiritual journalist, Joel Anastasi, and I, also present (live and through teleconference on a regular basis) *Divine Discussions* **gatherings at The Center for Spiritual Living, Ft. Lauderdale.** Either Jeff or I go into trance, *present a teaching or messages* from higher realms and then **open the endeavor up to the audience's questions and higher realm answers.** This **allows others direct access to these frequencies** so they may address core issues within their personal lives or the world at large. These higher realms have a way of '*reading' your Light body* and addressing what is needed in your life to achieve what you say you want.

Let us now go into some of the mechanics of exactly **how I became a channel** and see if it further assists you in becoming a channel. (Realizing each one of us has a unique path to the activation of our soul plans, our purpose in being here). My colleague Jeff preceded me in channeling by a couple of years. One day we were trading healing sessions (as trained Reiki and Light Ascension Therapists), and Jeff connected with the **Archangel Uriel** who said they had been attempting to gain my attention for some time to be a channel for their *band of consciousness*. I barely knew who Uriel was. Archangel Uriel gave me fifty days to decide if it resonated for me to be a channel for them, to mark my calendar with various exercises and to reach a decision at the end of the fifty days. The moment they asked I knew the answer was yes. Meanwhile, I did my research on Archangel Uriel and realized we had a lot in common. Many of these early Uriel channelings are in my book, *Man Power God Power*. I read them often and continue to be thrilled at the wisdom given to us. I am careful not to make these messages about me since I know they did not come from me but through me in service from whence they came.

DIVINE DISCUSSIONS

My Angel News Network colleagues and I were also asked by higher realms to be **proxies for humanity on two sacred journeys to the powerful vortex/portal of Mt. Shasta** to *perform higher realm instructed rituals* to assist our species within its Ascension Process of moving into a higher frequency of existence. Pretty heady stuff, but we brought plenty of our Earthly wounds and defenses with us. My book, *Coming Home To Lemuria, An Ascension Adventure Story*, recaps a full diary of these events. **When you read and perform the rituals in the book, you also become proxies for humanity.** This book has been adapted into a stage play (and later screen play) so that the wisdoms within this book can be brought further out into humanity through another form of human entertainment.

Let's go into more detail as to exactly how I channel and see if it supports you in channeling. I was blessed to have direct contact by Archangel Uriel within my initial channeling process, but this may not be your experience. Since each of us is unique, you will discover your path, which needs to be nothing like mine.

While some people just start channeling with no seeming preparation, there are some general variables that I think help. *One word of caution: no one needs to 'certify' you, or give you permission or teach you how to channel. If you are to channel higher realms, it is a component of your soul plan, and no one but you can take that away from you. Here are some circumstances that help me and others I know who channel:*

> 1. I make sure I am feeling well and not under the influence of any distractions.
>
> 2. I make sure that the physical surroundings are

cleared and peaceful and not open to any interruptions.

I take a few deep breaths and quiet my mental and emotional bodies as much as possible. My mantra is; "This is not about me, I release myself from myself and let go to receive the highest good from the higher realms." I pause and wait for the frequency to identify themselves (they speak in the plural "we"). If they are not willing to identify themselves, and explain their purpose in connecting, I do not go forward.

3. I repeat who the higher realm is to verify what I am receiving is correct.

4. In order to receive this higher frequency, since I am vibrating at a lower/dense frequency, I have to prepare (entrain) my body to receive a higher vibration. I do this by continuing to breathe deeply. The higher frequency also has to lower their vibration so I can accept them without any harm. So we are 'meeting' at a midway energy point that works for both of us. The higher realms know we channels cannot receive the full impact of their higher frequency without harm.

5. I can channel by hearing the message and writing it down (my books were written that way), or the higher realms can use my voice and body and speak through me. You will find your own path with this. Some of you may see the higher realm through a symbol or vision.

6. When the session is over, I usually ask others to leave me alone and allow themselves and me

to integrate what has come through. I do not need praise or comments after I channel since what has come through is not about me. I have simply been in service to that frequency. Many channels do not realize that they channel what they need within their soul plan; this is the divine balance of giving and receiving in being a channel.

7. Most of the frequencies I channel usually open with a basic message or teaching, and I am blessed that the majority of them open to questions and answers for more in-depth integration. Not all higher realm frequencies and channels open to questions and answers.

8. If someone has received a personal message by asking, "Do you have a message for me?" I often suggest that they listen to the audio later and to transcribe it to allow better integration.

To be the clearest channel you can be, I would also suggest that you be in a personal process of clearing any of your wounds and ego defenses. There are many gifted therapists out there. Use your resonance and discernment in finding them. Before I began channeling, I had been in a metaphysical therapeutic personal process for several years.

I was blessed to be trained in Reiki and Light Ascension by a very gifted higher realm trance channel. So channeling was not foreign to me, and I had experienced many channeling sessions before I began channeling.

No matter how or when it happens for you to channel,

please know it is your divine birthright to be and do so. Humanity is transcending into being multi-dimensional, and channeling is a key component in that. Humanity cannot transcend/advance without the support and love of these higher realms. We never could and cannot now. So open your hearts and minds to all the possibilities and probabilities that are waiting to come to you and for you to share with the world. **We have never been alone.**

To learn more about my channeling in its support of your channeling, please visit the web sites below, and also for our continued contact in building communities of equality, harmony and balance.

The Light Of Source Never Fails,

PhillipEltonCollins.com

TheAngelNewsNetwork.com

DIVINE DISCUSSIONS

Being Co-Creator: From Child To Adult

From: Your Creator.

Dear Beloved Daughters And Sons Being Human,

We are your Cosmic Mother and Father, a combination of the balanced universal divine feminine and masculine energies, coming to you at a crucial time within the evolution of your planet and species. Your destiny and birthright is to evolve into a higher state of consciousness by raising your vibrations/frequencies through a universal process called Ascension. **This will allow you to create a world of equality, harmony and balance through We Consciousness/Unity in order to be in world service** (moving from the unhealed me to the healed We). **An essential aspect of this process is you accepting, knowing and applying you being the co-creators of your existence.** You are a direct extension/child of your Cosmic Mother and Father, your Creator. You have many of our same powers within you, and your time of full self-empowerment has come. This is not unlike your Superman story where he discovers his original and true powers and how to use them for the good of all. There have been many forces within your paths to prevent you from knowing this truth -- especially your fear or disbelief of the Divine Power within you. The time of awaking is upon you!

Dear **Children of Creation** no matter how things appear in your outside world, and within yourself, you are transmuting from childhood to adulthood through the acceptance of you being Divine Beings, co-creating your reality. If you so choose, it is time to know we are **The Founding Family of Creation.** Throughout transitioning yourself from children to adults, you will transform your world into one of equality, harmony and balance. The mission of this planet to learn to love is being achieved through accepting with compassion our co-creatorship.

We fully understand that the reality of you as co-creators may be challenging for many. You have been taught otherwise for a long time. It may be an intellectual idea but not an actual truth. But a new teaching and learning is upon you, dear Children. You were originally created to be co-creators with the Divine, and that is what is awakening now. Through your present Ascension Process, you are coming to a complete comprehension of what and how being co-creators means.

You are joining your Divine Father, Mother and Family through your ownership of the reality of being co-creators. Through false teachings, you have been dumbed down to not remembering or knowing that all of what we speak of now is true. When you look at your outside world and many personal lives in constant upheaval of duality, separation, and confrontation, it is challenging to know you are who you are. But the mask of not knowing is dropping, dear Children. The governmental, religious, financial and personal challenges creating emotional, mental and physical imbalances can create a feeling of powerlessness. This allows a victimhood consciousness that can only be transformed through ownership (a way you have chosen to learn what you need to learn the way you need to learn it). Victimhood says you are a powerless outsider who can never transform your life and world. This outsider attitude creates an erroneous belief system that you are helpless. This feeling is what is creating the terrorism in your world today, reflected in inequality, environmental and energy issues. As an outsider, you remain personally or globally unaware of the people around you who can utilize your compassion and help, even if it's only for them to be heard.

Dear Children, you are disempowering yourselves rather than self-empowering yourselves by not participating in stopping the abuse of planet Earth, by not making wiser choices on who governs your world, holding leaders accountable for transparency and truth or not knowing you can comfort another who is in pain.

You are being bombarded with more information than ever before within your recorded history. Much of this is negative. This negativity and the addiction to the communication technology create a negative perception. Dear Children, your emotions and thoughts are creating your reality. Are your emotions joyful and your thoughts manifesting magic, or are you focusing on the next possible dilemma?

Here is the good news: no matter what your personal conscious level or spiritual consciousness, there is a co-creator DNA molecule within each of you that is an essential aspect of your Divine Birthright. This Divine aspect is always within you. Many forces throughout history attempted to access or control this birthright, but they cannot and will not. This **co-creator consciousness** is a living aspect of the planet and you upon and within it. It is through your emotions, thoughts and choices that we are continuously co-creating together. Your use of free will (something else no one can take away from you) is a limitless creative ingredient to the unchangeable Law of Cause and Effect. Each time you make a choice, together *We* activate a chain of events with both intended and unintended consequences (applying the cosmic equation: Responsibility = Consequence).

An essential aspect of the activation of your soul plans is that you are realizing there is a determination that governs the activity of physical life. The Law of Cause and Effect maintains and sustains the actions of material matter. There is an aspect of creation that is not determined by the Law of Cause and Effect. These two aspects exist within *We*, The Creator and you.

We, The Creator, have an impersonal aspect (called Divine Empowerment) that powers physical forces within the Universe. There is also a personal aspect of *We*, The Creator, as the Divine Mother and Father. This aspect has been identified as your I AM Presence, your consciousness within that is always aware. Dear Children, it is this awareness that views all that manifests inside and outside you. It is this awareness that reveals the non-determining aspect/dimension of life. You are in the third dimension of feelings, thoughts and physical bodies and within the process of ascending to higher dimensions of love and Light.

Your quantum sciences have begun to observe and further explore the interaction of the above dimensions through the study of the interaction of electrons and atoms. Natural sciences are beginning to intersect with spiritual science. You have learned that energetic forces behavior cannot always be predicted without factoring in awareness/consciousness; it is the same with you. Many of your choices cannot be predetermined since you are gifted with free choice and will. It is your free will and choice that prevents predetermination. *We*, The Creator, do not interfere with your future choices, but once you determine a choice the Laws of the Universe determine the effect of your actions/choices. If you cannot follow this, simply know within your hearts, dear Children, all is in *Divine Order*. There are many Laws and Equations keeping all of Creation in balance. It is your destiny to eventually master them all.

It is your free will and choice that eternally connects us to our co-creative reality. So, dear Children, what will *We* co-create together? How about a world of equality, harmony and balance where you become the master teachers of your world in full service to one another and the world!

If you remember only one thing from this message and teaching, let it be, know and understand it is your Divine Birthright to be in full co-creative relationship with the forces that created you. We are expressions of one another. Whether you are aware of it or not, you are already creating your life within each and every hour of the now. So *We* ask you, "What type of life is it that you say you want? What kind of life are you actually creating now? What kind of life can we create together tomorrow?"

In reality, dear Children, it is not what happens to you in life (as a learning tool you are choosing) but how you choose in your free will to respond. Within your soul plan's limitless creative capacity, you are always co-creating past, present and future into the now, allowing another choice. When you are not sure what you need to do, do what you can, dear Children, and then hand it over to *We* in higher realms; let go and hand it off to your Co-Creator!

As we began this message/teaching, *We* realize your

world is experiencing a great clearing and cleansing from inequality and lack of harmony and balance. Look out in your world and begin to realize that your needs are the same (even those who seem so different) and there is plenty for all. Realize, dear Children, that change is a process of your healing from the inside out and bringing that healed you out into the world. **Our making the world a peaceful, loving place is our true Co-Creatorship!** There are many tools and teachings coming to you from higher realms. You are not powerless. Are you ready to apply them?

Dear Children, true healing begins with nurturing by allowing yourself and others to be heard in order to awaken your divine, authentic sense of self. You and your world are divinely changing. It is your destiny to do so. Together, *We* are building a better tomorrow that you and your children can come back to. **Can you see everything about you and your world as a reflection of what needs to change and how** *We* **are being/doing this as a Co-Creation?**

Things will change when each and every one of you help create the change. You are all responsible for the past and present which becomes the future, which becomes the now. Where and when do you wish to take our conscious Co-Creation, dear Children? **Remember, you are Divine Children of Creation becoming adult of a loving Creator.** *We* are bringing higher consciousness spirit into the Earth together. Our collective creation is within our hearts and hands. What do you choose as you move from childhood to adulthood?

Being Human

From: Archangel Uriel, World Teacher And Guardian

Dear Beloved Humans Choosing To Be Human,

Being Human (humanity being God and God being humanity), is a divinely supported self-balancing-correcting personal process that allows, through your freedom of choice and will, to forego (transmute) being human and returning to cosmic BEingness: pure Light from whence you came. You are in the process of mastering The Laws of BEingness.

Can you now fully forgive yourselves for choosing to learn the way you choose to learn in order to forgive others, since you are all one? Once this takes place, you have freed yourselves from yourselves and can move into world and universal service, your purpose in being here.

Alphabetical Listing Of Articles: C

Changing Your Comprehension Of Change
Coming Home To Your BEingness
Competition
Considering Karma
Council Of Creation
Creating Community With Creation

Changing Your Comprehension Of Change

From: Akashic Record.

You might be familiar with the phrase *change is all there is*. What exactly does this mean, and what is change's relationship with the world and yourselves? What is the meaning, value and purpose of change? Let us tap into the cosmic wisdom of the Akashic Record and see what clarity this universal library of knowledge and change can bring.

Ever since the creation of planet Earth (see *A New Creation Story* on page 4) and the origin of humanity, there has been nothing but change. Humanity is within the Ascension Process of learning the truth of the origin of the planet and itself. You only have a piece of the puzzle at present and soon you shall be ready to receive the true, complete history of the beginning of planet Earth and those within and upon it. This teaching is beginning to be presented to humanity and will create the greatest change ever in your world.

As stated, since the beginning of the world there has been nothing but change; this is also true for your human physical bodies made of the same atoms and energy as the planet. You have been taught that every few years you actually create new cells within your physical body, thus a new you. This is a signal of your true immortal state-of-being. In reality you can never die, just change physical bodies between lives (while maintaining the same spiritual being). Someday this physical body shifting will change as you are destined to become immortal beings living in the same energetic bodies forever growing and expanding.

Change can often feel like chaos. **Chaos is an essential aspect of creation, which is comprised of construction and destruction.** There is always a breakdown followed by a breakthrough in creating the new. Change is all about changing from the old to the new world and you. Actually, stored within DNA cells are the memory of the creation of this world and you. You are learning how to access this wisdom by moving from unconsciousness to consciousness (waking up).

As the Earth clears and cleanses herself through change (geomagnetic activities), so do humans through a personal process of knowing who they are and why they are here (a process of inside out). Change for humanity is the way showing humanity's ultimate pathway back into Divinity; man power becoming God Power (refer to *Man Power God Power* by this author).

Human emotions, thoughts and thus activities are also responsible for many Earth changes such as the creation of weather and some geological events. These are stored in the atmosphere and interior of the planet. Once these energies reach critical mass, they create an event, a change. Humanity is now waking up to their energetic correlation between the planet and themselves. Both individual and collective consciousness are learning tools allowing humanity to learn the lessons they need to learn. You are, indeed, one: planet and humanity.

There have been several golden ages (Lemuria, Atlantis, Egypt, Mayan, Aztec, etc.) on this planet that have been stepping stones of change to humanity's final destination of evolving into a higher state of being into We Consciousness/Unity. Each past golden age slowly allowed humanity to wake up through the change of growth and expansion. Again, the greatest change is through a personal process (inside out) of loving self and mirroring that love to others and the planet. This change has been called the activation of soul plans (your reason to be here).

The time has come for the planet (as we) to return to the Light from whence it came (the destiny of all planets). This is the grandest change of all! Thus all within and upon the planet are given the choice through free will to do the same. This journey/change back to the Light (Divinity) is the personal process responsibility of each individual moving inside out to Love and Oneness. No one can be forced to do this and no one can do it for us.

So all the change humanity experiences, within many lifetimes on planet Earth, is not about changing the planet but changing/transforming yourselves, moving from the wounded me to the healed We. Humanity has often forgotten the purpose in being here or remembering who they are (Divine Beings having a human experience) or knowing why they are here (to learn to love). All the changing events in the world and your personal lives are to remind you of who you are and why you are here. Humanity's Divine Destiny/evolution responds by stimulating consciousness/awareness, thus change.

Let humanity no longer give power away to governments, religions, and corporations but have these organizations reflect self-empowerment and love of self and one another, creating communities of equality, harmony and balance. All the global terrorism and upheaval at present in the world is a cry to bring humanity together and to help one another through change. There is enough for everyone! Let this be your common ideal in spite of cultural, religious, racial or gender differences.

What affects one, affects all. Imbalances through abusing planet Earth or separation amongst yourselves radiates out throughout the solar system, galaxy and universe. A divine relationship exists between humanity and *All There Is* that requires the application of Universal Laws of Love. Since you came from and are Divinity, you are asked to be Divine. **When you are out of balance with Creation, change is created to bring you back into balance, so you can change yourselves and thus your world.**

The changing events in your world and your lives today are to enable humanity to remember who they are and why they are here. The purpose of change is to mirror the shift taking place within the planet herself (returning to Light and Love). Humanity and Mother Earth, as one being, are changing, growing and expanding in consciousness of self and its relationship with Creation.

DIVINE DISCUSSIONS

Coming Home To Your BEingness

From: Beings of Cosmic Consciousness.

Dear Beloved Human Beings, Being Human And Beyond,

We are the Beings of Cosmic Consciousness, and our eternal home is the Akashic Records, the Halls of Wisdom containing all knowledge. Our Earthly home is your higher being, your non-physical sacred soul, the aspect of you that is One with *All There Is*.

Many of your personal lives and world events are involved within a process of evolution through chaos and upheaval. This is the '**old**' of your life and world that is screaming to move into the **'new'**. We come at this time of great change to remind you of an innate *state of BEing, a cosmic awareness* that can be your *pathway to the new*....creating the life you say you want.

The fact that this Cosmic/Divine aspect of you really exists is an ancient memory for many, and the intention of this reminder is to further awaken you so that you can once again **access being cosmically conscious**. Remember, you are a Divine Spiritual Being choosing to have this human being experience, so it should be no surprise that this Divine Part of you actually exists. You are Creation experiencing itself, so how could it be otherwise?

Creation has no intention of abandoning you in your choice of choosing to be human. For those who choose through freedom of will and choice to create newness in your life, **we welcome you to the pathway to that new life**...

So let us begin to discuss you becoming One with the Beings of Cosmic Consciousness, you, in effect, becoming Cosmic Consciousness. Many of you are not exactly sure what this is, so let us use the limitations of human language, words, and see if we can shed some further enlightenment on this.

Let us start with your human emotions, your emoted feelings, as a way to describe this higher aspect of you. Have you ever had a dream in which you feel like you are everywhere at the same time? That you are One with everything when you are standing in a silent forest? In this dream, or forest, you sense you can now understand the interrelationships of all things and there is a clarity and all-knowing wisdom that wasn't previously there. When this first happens, it may be only for a split second, but in that second you know you are changed forever and intend to spend more time in this *state of being* as soon as you can. You are promised by this state of being the more times you go there the longer you can stay next time. You may access this place in the silence of meditation and by focusing on your breath.

Through ascension energies coming into your planet at this time, via various geographic portals/vortices, you will have increased access to this all-knowing higher aspect of yourself with more grace and ease and more often, if you so choose. This is also what has happened in the past when your inventors, scholars and great philosophers received needed wisdoms to advance the human species at special times of dispensation. Yes, they 'received' through accessing their Cosmic Consciousness; they did not think things up through their brain. The human brain is a receiver of higher frequency data.

DIVINE DISCUSSIONS

The timing of your various incarnational cycles, along with the ascension energies, also affects your ability to access this higher aspect of self (reflecting *All There Is*). Some of you have needed many lifetimes to achieve the ability of which we speak. During this special time of moving into a higher frequency of existence (ascension), your believing minds are moving back into service to your knowing hearts. This allows you to 'think' with your hearts insuring positive intentions for what you seek, insuring no intention of harm. Any negative or dense energy will prevent access to your higher state of being. There is no exerting any human wounds or ego defenses into this higher all-knowing aspect of self.

Through the Ascension Process and by increasing your consciousness, you are raising your frequency/vibrational rate. Your Cosmic Consciousness lives in a high frequency of existence, and you need to reach it in order to access your higher self. Some will not be able to achieve this higher state without a deep examination of self through a personal process. Such higher realm tools are available to you from many endeavors such as the one this channel helped create: The Angel News Network. If you are one who needs more personal growth and expansion, know that all the support you need awaits you from higher realms such as Archangels, Angels, Ascended Masters, Inner Earth Civilizations, Galactic Forces and the Star Systems that seeded your planet. Many of you are choosing to directly connect with these realms and bring their needed wisdoms to humanity.

Through your personal process, you will awaken to fully know *who you are* and *why you are here* and become able to apply your talents and gifts out into the world.

All of this will be achieved through a healed loving relationship with self -- reflected to others and your world. As you continue this self-work, you will surely be able to access your Cosmic Consciousness connection through the frequency of Oneness. You will be moving from 'me consciousness' to 'We Consciousness' into Oneness.

All of this is actually you **activating your Divine Soul Plan**, your reason and purpose in being here. This world would be incomplete without each and every one of you, and you are beginning to embrace this truth and trust it through self-love mirrored inside out. You will begin to know you are here to serve one another and the world by supporting and loving it all. The activation of your soul plan is your spiritual journey, and you will achieve it when it is right for your plan; you are not in control of that which you did not create. The thing you can be and do along the way is to keep increasing your vibration by your personal work to match the higher consciousness aspect of you that you intend to access.

You have created many 'learning tool' experiences along the pathway of this lifetime that have brought you to this moment of now. The world you are living in at present needs all of your assistance to advance within its Earthly soul plan of transmuting into a higher frequency of existence (as you are also). You are all here to master self (as a reflection of *All There Is*) and move into world service through creating communities of equality, harmony and balance (there is not much of that in your present world). You can become a *Consultant To Change* by becoming more conscious of your emotions and thoughts that are creating actions not supporting the good of all. Connecting with your

DIVINE DISCUSSIONS

Cosmic Consciousness will greatly assist you.

Your Cosmic Consciousness is *housed* within the eternal limitlessness of *All There Is*, Oneness. There is no time nor space here where all the wisdom of everything exists. The problem is much of humanity, not even your most gifted intellectuals, often do not see themselves good nor worthy enough to know how to access this arena. The emotions within the emotional body and the thoughts within the human mental body can sabotage self. It is this you are in the personal process of learning how to heal. But once you connect with your higher self-consciousness, just once, all fear, doubt and ignorance (the monsters of mankind) disappear. **You know you have come home to your true** *Divine Destiny Of BEingness*.

Once connected to your *Divine Destiny Of BEingness* you will know Oneness by experiencing you as one with all things. Previously, the concept of Oneness was something trapped within your mental body: now it has transcended to your knowing heart, and you begin to think with your heart. As you enter into your *selfless Oneness* more often, any and all boundaries into it will dissolve and all that had been hidden will be revealed. You will become skilled at applying your attention and intention into manifesting exactly what you say you want (with no intention of harm and for the good of all).

Within the higher state of your BEingness is the true you, the conscious/fully awakened you without limits, connected to all cosmic wisdom. You soon realize that being human, **being a human being, is a tiny part of your Eternal Consciousness** that is constantly growing and expanding -- you have become true BEingness transitioning into Divine doingness. You, in effect, become connected to the Light from whence you came by being 'enlightened.' Creation is a process of becoming enlightened, returning to the Light. You came from Light, chose density (by lowering your vibration/frequency) as a way to learn, and now you are returning to Light (increasing your frequency/vibration). The circle of creation is complete in order to start over any way you choose.

Your Eternal Divine Soul has no issues with comprehending your Cosmic Consciousness through Oneness. It is your human self that may forget and needs a little nudge every now and then. The truth of your being lives within the DNA of your heart. When you forget the true you, forgive yourself and *think with your heart.* Cosmic Love chambered within your heart will always show you the way home.

Competition

From: Archangel Uriel, World Teacher And Guardian.

Dear Humans Being Human,

When you evolve into our realms, you will lose the need to be on competitive teams or to have someone 'have your back.' Your team and back will be your Oneness. Your present competitive 'sports' are an exaggerated extension of your assertive masculine energy. Your 'professional sports' are largely a deceit controlled by monetary gain, power and harming the players at the expense of entertaining others. What some of you individually experienced was often the inclusion and exclusion of others. Competition leading to winning and losing is a form of duality and separation that you are destined to heal. Forgive yourselves for being and choosing to be human and learning the way you have chosen. Know you are in the process of ascending into a higher state of being human that does not include that of which we speak.

Competition is merely an extension of your separation, which can lead to confrontation (a non-balancing of the feminine and masculine energies). Needing to be on a competitive team is the wounded little boy or girl, through their herd consciousness, saying, "love me, let me belong, let me be good enough." Dear ones, you are in the process of learning to love self, thus others, and not needing competition or teams of inclusion and exclusion.

We would be happy to discuss and process this with you at length, if need be. We have initiated the conversation as an aspect of your growth and expansion.

Considering Karma

From: Akashic Record.

Dear Fellow Humans Being Human,

Throughout spiritual and metaphysical teachings, there is much mention of karma, an iconic word that is often misunderstood and misused. Let us pull some wisdom from the Akashic Record and see if we can achieve more clarity regarding this wondrous learning tool.

From *God's Glossary: A Divine Dictionary,* the Akashic Record is defined as: "a complete cosmic record of all the wisdom of the universe; this planet's soul plan (reason to be) and our individual soul plan are housed within this hall of wisdom; humanity is in the process of learning how to access this record stored in higher realms; some are now able to access and share this information."

Let us together take a deep breath, connect with this record on high, and see what truth can be revealed regarding karma. As with all information received, please use your resonance and discernment within the receiving and giving of this information.

Some see karma in a rather negative light, mere fate, or a punishment from the past creating a feeling of helplessness. Karma is not often seen as a learning tool to assist humanity within its evolutionary journey to rediscover its Divinity. The forces of Creation are not here to punish, judge or harm but to keep humanity and the universe within balance.

Your many incarnations on planet Earth are simply

pathways of awakening and self-empowerment. This includes karma which has been created to empower not disempower. Actually, karma is a remembrance stored within the DNA cellular memory of human hearts and passed on from lifetime to lifetime. So, in effect, karma is not a lack or limitation. It is a soul plan memory activated by life's emotions, thoughts, thus energy. It can be as supportive and loving as it can be consequential and challenging.

So the concept of karmic debt or 'karma is a bitch' could be replaced with seeing karma as a personal processing – attachment - memory that you can choose through your freedom of choice and will to factor into your life, or not, in order to learn from it and release it. This attachment could be to a person, place or thing that no longer serves your highest good or soul plan. Karma is often an unconscious attachment that becomes conscious. So, in fact, there is no such thing as karmic debt, just the personal karmic remembrance that you can choose to release after learning from it what you need to learn (being worthy or good enough).

Another way to better understand and explain karma is to show similar aspects elsewhere reflected in your BEingness. Showing the perfection in all Creation, karma is actually rather similar to your own body's integration process. In the same way you take in air, water or food and assimilate it, creating an either positive or negative effect, your energetic/etheric bodies 'digest' karmic remembrances stored within cellular memories by the present life experiences/consequences it attracts.

In reality, past life experiences, talents and gifts come back to you in the present since they are stored within your cellular memory from lifetime to lifetime.

Sometimes you resume uncompleted negative and positive relationships and see talents and gifts from a previous life come into the present; an example would be prodigies. A wonderful explanation of addiction is that it is created by unexpressed negative emotions expressed in the next lifetime. Some of this can prevent the full activation of the soul plan (your reason to be here): this requires knowing who you are and why you are here. There are many teachings from higher realms to assist humanity in answering these who and why questions.

Ultimately, all these memories will be examined and resolved in order to create a shift in consciousness or an awakening of the self. It is essential to remember that even what you may call negative karmic memories are not basically right or wrong, good or bad. They are only memories, and you are not your memories. These memories are (not so simply) learning tools to learn what you need to learn the way you need to finally learn once and for all. Whether your memories lead to positive or negative consequences is a matter of your freedom of choice and will; this is the most essential aspect of how you actually deal with the memory.

Freedom of will and choice is a human component that no one can take from you, a 'gift from the gods' learning tool. For, in reality, the choices you make through your free will determine an outcome, not karma.

Please remember, the golden goal of the 'Laws Of Karma' is simply growth and expanded consciousness; waking up and remembering who you are (spiritual beings having a human experience) and knowing why you are here (to learn to love self, others and your world) in order to be in world service. You can do this through grace and ease, if you so choose.

Let us now create a new definition of karma and add it to *God's Glossary: A Divine Dictionary. Karma is not a debt; it is not a punishment. It simply is an interchange of memory energy that your soul plan draws upon through experiencing all of life; positive karmic memories awaken your talents and gifts; negatives ones can call for a shift in behavior/consciousness.*

As humanity enters the final 2,000-year Ascension cycle for this planet (returning to the Light from whence you came), remember, life is a divine ever-unfolding personal process of growth and expansion leading to Oneness, thus Divinity.

The Light of Source Never Fails.

Council Of Creation

From: Council of Creation.

Dear Beloved Humans Choosing To Be Human,

The intention of this message is to introduce ourselves to humanity at this most important juncture within your evolutionary path. To simply know of our existence can change your reality, if you choose.

We are The Council of Creation in service to *All There Is/God/Source* come to you through your I AM Presence and Christ Consciousness energies, your Eternal Divine BEingness.

We are the bands-of-consciousness and energies through which your Divinity (connection to your Eternal Higher Selves) is maintained and sustained, dear ones. We come to you to support your process of what you call Ascension: moving into your destined higher frequency/vibration of existence.

What exactly does this mean? You are an Eternal BEing of Light that has chosen THROUGH CHOOSING TO BE HUMAN to forget at times that you are a Being of Light reflecting *All There Is*. The purpose of this (and the way you are choosing to learn through your freedom of choice and will) is so that you never forget again, which you have done many times in your past.

You are in the process of remembering and applying who you truly are and knowing why you are here (as are we, at The Council of Creation), to be in service to all Creation, beginning for you with world service. You have chosen to be all aspects of being human; that includes all aspects of 'what is not' in order to fully know and apply 'what is.' This is the only way the human soul could imprint the needed truth in order to transcend into Eternal Spirit.

Let us further give examples of how the above process is taking place within your history and present existence.

First and foremost, dear Humanity, please know and remember humanity is not in control of the existence of your reality or the universe. You cannot control what you did not create. You have a given Divine Soul Plan as a species to return to higher realms of existence from whence you came. You are in the process of returning to higher realms through your freedom of choice and will (a gift and learning tool from Creation). We at The Council of Creation are observing the often folly of humanity through your choices, full acceptance, compassion and forgiveness, for this process allows transcending the process. If it resonates, we ask now that you begin to look deeply at your past and present choices in order to see, through wisdom (applied knowledge), if you wish to begin to make other choices, which reflect your Divinity.

Dear Ones, you all came from the same Source with the same needs, created from the same eternal elements. When are you going to see this Oneness and know we have created enough for all of you without your further attempting to control that which you did not create? You have created duality, separation and often confrontation (as a learning tool), which in reality do not actually exist. When are you going to choose to wake up from this insanity?

As you have moved further and further from the truth,

in order to maintain and sustain your Divinity, humanity has received from our Council dispensations to allow your shift to higher frequencies of existence. As at present, there have been many times in your human history when you have chosen to separate from the higher realms that have maintained and sustained your past advanced civilization through the connection to *All There Is*.

Much of your true history and evolution as a species is unknown. Those attempting to control you have often kept it from you. It is time (if you so choose) to know and apply your true evolutionary process in order to prevent your history continuing to repeat itself. It is time, if you so choose, to stop the karmic wheel of cause and effect, duality/separation and life and death and step into your true format of Eternal Divine Formless BEingness. The time-line of this is upon you dear humans. You are entering the final phase of learning the way you have in the past and awakening and allowing the true you to appear. This is your destiny no matter how things may appear in your world today. The forces at play, at present, are clearing and cleansing all the unhealed aspects of humanity that have caused your inequality, non-harmony and imbalance.

Let us give some examples of the past, many of which are not known or accepted by humanity. The intention, dear ones, is to not continue to repeat the past. You have had many past 'golden ages' (supported by higher realms) upon this divine learning laboratory of love, planet Earth. These civilizations achieved much more than you have at present. As many of you know, the purpose of the creation of this planet is to learn to love (the building block of all Creation) and apply that love within the creation of a world of Unity Consciousness. This is a preparation for joining we at The Council of Creation in service to *All There Is*.

Lemuria, Atlantis, early Egypt, Aztec, Mayan (and several other civilizations before and after), existed on your planet as a result of their connection to the higher realms -- Archangelic Realms (servicing humanity), Star Systems (seeded the creation of your planet), Inter-Galactic (from other solar systems), Ascended Masters (who once walked the Earth) and Inner Earth (who once resided upon the Earth surface). Each of these civilizations reached a point of advancement beyond where you are now due to their connection and support of higher realms.

Each of these advanced civilizations failed due to their disconnect from the higher realms that maintained and sustained them. The human mind (through its freedom of choice and will) thought it could be and do it a better way. As a result of the higher realms disconnect, many of these civilizations went into interior and external conflict/wars, not unlike your recent patterns of behavior. As a result of their advanced weaponry, the surface of the planet became an unpleasant place to sustain life. Many civilizations were then given dispensation through our Council to shift to a higher frequency of existence and create a new reality, a higher vibrational world within the core/interior of planet Earth. The purpose of this action is so that humanity will have a sustained path to its destiny/destination of Divinity. At present, unknown to most of humanity on the surface, there are many advanced civilizations within the core of planet Earth supporting your advancement on the surface. The goal is that when humanity on the surface is conscious enough, the two inner and surface worlds will join in Oneness (fully connected to higher realms) in order to advance the evolutionary process of humanity as a whole.

The channel we are coming through at present and his brethren at The Angel News Network are evolutionary members of The Great White Brotherhood in service to this Council. The energies of the I AM Presence and Christ Consciousness (your Eternal Higher Selves) empower this brethren-hood and are the God-given tools of this Council of Creation.

We Are In Eternal Support and Love of Humanity.

Creating Community With Creation

From: Cosmic Keepers of Creation.

Dear Humans Being Human,

We, the Cosmic Keepers of Creation, accessing the Akashic Records, come to you at this crucial time within your evolutionary path to discuss the significance of choosing to connect with the forces of Creation called God, Creator, Source, *All There Is* (or whatever name of which you resonate).

The truth is all of your past Golden Ages (Lemuria, Atlantis, Egypt, Aztec, and Mayan) and the creation of this final Golden Age are maintained and sustained by higher realms forces from whence you originated. **Your choice to separate from forces of Creation, and/or abusing higher realm powers, has been the cause and effect of much of the pain and suffering in your world.**

At this time of ascension of your planet and humanity (evolving into a higher frequency of existence) the essential connection with the forces of Creation are coming to the forefront again. Many of your sciences are now co-mingling with universal/cosmic truths, allowing a deeper **connection between humanity, Creation and consciousness itself.** You are once again bringing Creation down from the cosmos into your knowing hearts, transmuting Creation from some masculine God-figure *up there* to an essential aspect and divine expression of each human being. It is crucial that you reach this profound development within your personal processing at this time.

The big question that the human mind asks is:

"What is the purpose of the creation of humanity?"

Your understanding and accepting the answer is the key that unlocks the door to knowing who you are and why you are here. Creation (*God/Source/All There Is*) created you, as a reflection of itself, to create communities of equality, harmony and balance. This is developed through learning to love self and mirror that out into world service; in effect, creating relationships based upon Love. Since Love is the building block of all Creation, you are learning to be the Creator. You already are creating your lives; they just may not be what you say you want, since you have not yet mastered learning and being Love.

You have been evolving on this planet for eons in an unconsciousness of '*sleeping spiritual slumber,*' which has created the lack and limitation, duality and confrontation leading to pain moving into suffering. Through self-imposed fear, doubt and ignorance you have not remembered how to create your lives as Divine Beings having a human being experience. Many of you are waking up, have had enough of not remembering and **have called forth creating community with Creation.**

Creating community with Creation, true spirituality, is a simple concept that the human mind loves to complicate through thinking it has a better way. Some religions have altered your reality and controlled you for a long time. Many creation and spirituals books are written by people who know nothing of True Creation or spirituality. **It has been the blind leading the blind.** Time to wake up and see, if you so choose.

Creating a community with Creation, true spirituality, **is**

a state of being, a divine state of consciousness that allows equality, harmony and balance, through love. This state of BEingness, as a foundation, allows doingness to reflect the highest good of all. Your present social norms, religious endeavors and governments *(that you are so eager to give your power away to)* do not reflect a divine state of BEingness. Are you ready to make another choice in connecting with your Divine Essence and reflect that out into your world?

The purpose of this message is to bring a simple tool to humanity to assist you in creating community with Creation, a brother/sisterhood that reflects your Divine Essence, creating a new world paradigm of We Consciousness. *Creation never intended to be separate from humanity.* Humanity separated all on your own, thinking you had a better way. **Creation's intent is to bring an awareness of the divine into physicality, thus into your three dimensional world of emotions and thoughts.**

Know this, dear one: Creation actually needs you (humanity) in the never-ending evolution of creation. That's how essential each and every one of you is or you would not be here!

We can hear the human mind now saying, "And why would all powerful Creation/God need humanity in any way?" Dear ones, it has to be and do with **Love and Oneness.** Your Eternal Divine Souls were created out of Creation's desire/intent for community. **The mechanics of Creation is, ultimately, connection with the rest of Creation, and that includes you.** Connection and love can only be experienced in relationship to other beings. This is why learning to love self is so essential to allowing loving community with Creation, loving God, loving you. Your experience mirrors back to Creation, allowing conscious reality. Your experience of what you feel and think of reality is actually a mirrored reflection of your true reality as experiences in consciousness. The delineation between creative reality outside self and the human reality inside one's self affects your relationship with Creation. **Creating community with Creation is a process of learning to love inside out, not outside in.** This is why learning the importance of the loving relationship with self is so essential to loving others and creating communities of equality, harmony and balance with Creation.

One of the most challenging aspects for humanity, in creating community with Creation, is to know and accept that you are spiritual beings having a human experience. This requires moving from the mind that wishes to hold on to the physical third dimensional world rather than move into your loving heart that knows your Eternal Spiritual BEing. **You are not physical beings having a spiritual experience; you are spiritual beings being human.** You are not attempting to become something else that is not already within you; you are already spiritual beings (in spite of what you have been taught or forgot in the past). Your heart has all this truth stored within it; it is time to fully access the truth, *to think with your heart* (as the heart moves into service to the mind).

You have been taught or forgotten you originated in community with Creation, as **Children of Creation**. You have had so many lifetimes where you believed your physical earthly lives was all there is; you simply no longer remember from whence you came. Your soul plan at this time is to bring the community of Creation back into the earth plane. Many have been taught or believe that the mission is to get out of the Earth plane. Dear ones, Creation has been expressing itself through you all the time. You and Creation are co-mingled. You are in the process of learning to co-exist and merge with Creation so that the Divine will manifest through you. The truth of being in community with Creation is an essential aspect of your Ascension Process now, not something that happens when you reach enlightenment or after your so called death. **Your mission is to heal the wounds and ego defenses that have kept you in lack and limitation and separate from Creation. There are many teachings and tools available to you through endeavors such as The Angel News Network and other sources to assist you in completing your mission.**

Acknowledging and surrendering to higher realm greater wisdoms and guidance is essential. Through your personal process, your wounds and defenses are released, and you become receptive (eliminating resistance) to assimilating the community with Creation into your emotional, mental and physical bodies. **In effect, you begin to experience the community of Creation with all your bodies by becoming it.**

Each of you has within yourselves the innate **embryo of consciousness** of the community of Creation passed on from lifetime to lifetime. Right now is the time for the **birthing**, if you so choose. Your human heart has always known of the Divine Community Of Creation. The way to access all of which we speak is through your knowing heart, *to think with your heart.* **The purpose of your heart is to know you are One with the community of Creation; thus to experience the intimate/personal aspect of Creation.**

We of Creation define ourselves as that reality that is the Source of the universal experience of being, the *I AM Presence/experience.* You are beginning to realize there is an intersection where we meet. That place is within your heart containing your I AM Presence. Take a deep breath, and repeat after us. "I AM CREATION CREATING."

Welcome to Creating Community with Creation!

We, the Cosmic Keepers of Creation, by Creation, for Creation.

DIVINE DISCUSSIONS

Alphabetical Listing Of Articles: E

Eight Sacred Principles Of Leadership
Ever Lasting Energy

Eight Sacred Principles Of Leadership

From: Council of Archangelic Realms (CAR).

Dear Humans Being Human,

At this time, we shall present *Eight Sacred Principles of Leadership* that are largely missing in your world and are employed within advanced civilizations and higher realms. They will greatly assist you to move into a higher state of consciousness and allow your BEingness to create your doingness when you choose to employ these within your world.

1. Leaders need to be involved in a continuous process of self-mastery/knowledge. Most of your leaders today do not know their purpose in being here (who they are, why they are here) and are involved in selfish or controlling hidden pursuits.

2. Leaders need to fully know and apply the true nature/purpose of leadership: to be in compassionate world service. Most of your leaders today are all about the 'me' and not the 'we.'

3. Leaders need to apply the concepts of Unity Consciousness, knowing the interconnectedness of all things into Oneness. Your present leaders are largely not aware of the integration of all things on this planet; what affects one affects all.

4. Leaders need to know their home planet is a living,

conscious being, and they are stewards of their home. With all your concern about weather change and energy alternatives, who is speaking of this?

5. Leaders apply learned knowledge into wisdom by knowing what has not worked in the past. Your present leaders still believe killing one another in war and attempting to control what you did not create is acceptable.

6. Leaders know how to create conscious teams to manifest new realties. Your leaders today do not know how to effect collective positive change for all, realizing change is all there is.

7. Leaders know no one individual is in charge and understand the nature of pluralism. Your present leaders are often motivated by individual greed, wounds and ego defenses.

8. Leaders need to fully understand, be responsible and accountable for their actions. Many of your leaders today are working within fear, doubt and ignorance.

Ever Lasting Energy

From: Akashic Records.

At this time, let us discuss the type of energy that is responsible for maintaining and sustaining all life: energy that is responsible for humanity being telepathic, an energy that moves far beyond the individual connecting everything. How this energy works is one of the key elements missing in most natural sciences' awareness of the human being.

Everything on and in planet Earth has an energetic frequency, which connects to the frequency that matches it. Energy flows in the direction of and connects with the energy that attracts it; this is from the **Law of Attraction** from Archangel Uriel. Humanity's consciousness creates a field of attraction that magnetizes energy, allowing corresponding energetic frequencies to attach themselves to humanity.

Many spiritual and metaphysical wisdoms now teach that humanity is rising (ascending) increasing vibrations (frequency/energy) to achieve a higher state of consciousness/BEingness, moving from the wounded, dualistic me consciousness to unified, healed We Consciousness/Oneness. This is humanity's destiny as they evolve from a dense carbon based reality to a higher energy Light-based body. This rising of human energy is consistent with what is taking place within the planet itself, an Ascension Process of returning to the high energy of Light from whence humanity came: this being the divine cycle of all planets. Thus, everything within and upon the planet, including humanity, will become the same high-energy frequency/vibration.

Humans are given a lifetime supply of energy during each incarnational cycle. What they do with this energy, through freedom of choice and will (their BEingness), is up to each human. *God's Glossary: A Divine Dictionary defines energy as a divine and unfailing source with no limit, an inherent power; all things are comprised of energy; energy is the basis of everything; eternal; the vitality of God and humanity, and all life; all powerful and empowering; everything is energy; creates spiritual and physical power; core of all existence; cannot be destroyed.*

Also during each lifetime, humans have the choice to activate their soul plan, their reason to be here, with the energy given. In effect, there is an interconnection between an individuated soul plan and the personal energy/vibration configuration. This energy pattern is as unique as eye corneas or fingerprints, since each person is a unique expression of Creation, knowing the universe would be incomplete without each and every human.

Emotions and thoughts activate the energy given to each human, creating their reality all the time. Emotions and thoughts create vibrations, which are a physical activity with an energetic effect that humans can experience. These vibrations contain information that human senses can actually read. When around other people, humans can read one another's 'vibes' whether they are positive or negative. These energetic vibrations create the personality traits of an individual. Telepathic, silent communication transports on the wavelengths of these vibrations, as well as long distance healing. On an energetic subconscious level what affects one, affects all. **This is the energetic basis of Oneness.** Quantum theories are in the process of understanding the role of consciousness (bands of energy) in the relationship between energy and physical matter. The awareness of humans as divine expressions of power and worthiness attracts higher frequencies that manifest as happiness, joy, peace and abundance. So humans create what they focus on. Become more conscious of what you choose to focus on, remembering the God Power within you. What you often fear most within you is this power.

What is taking place is that emotional and mental patterns precipitate energy into material manifestations. In effect, *when energy combines with emotions and thoughts creation takes place*. Natural sciences have yet to confirm what is known in ancient wisdoms; physical objects have a database of information contained in the energetic influences. Energetic vibrations can actually become a part of physical surroundings as a sort of residue. Have you ever walked into a room and felt uncomfortable there? Or picked up an object and felt strange or joyful about it? Negative energy/vibrations can be cleared by energy exercises, breathing techniques, washing, and positive ones received and enjoyed. **(Find some of the most complete and powerful energetic exercises in** *The Second Coming, Archangel Gabriel Proclaims A New Age*, **page 326, by Joel D. Anastasi, trance channeled by Robert Baker.).**

The most essential aspect of energy for the individual is its use within soul growth and expansion, the activation of the soul plan (the reason to be here). Through the activation of the soul plan, via the energies of emotions and thoughts, the individual discovers who they are and why they are here. Talents and gifts are revealed and projected out into the world through a loving relationship with self. All of this becomes a self-empowered transformation of embracing your higher self, allowing service to others and the planet through Universal Laws and Truths. A new awareness/consciousness of living spirit energy then becomes part of everyday life.

Through raised consciousness, a personal transformation introduces the Oneness of all life, a love and tolerance for all, as well as an acceptance, compassion and forgiveness for all erroneous belief systems, including all religions. The energetic activation of the soul plan becomes a template for individual growth and development through the raised personal energy/vibration and raised consciousness.

The energy given within each lifetime allows three essential tools for soul plan activations: (1) knowing the truth; who you are and why you are here; (2) the entrainment of the energy becoming application; and (3) the readiness to commit to using the energy for the highest good of self and others.

Becoming aware of any **disruption of energy** serves to bring you clarity. Out of chaos comes creation. Teaching tools are often disguised in a disruption of energy. Humanity is here to learn and grow. This can be possible from joy or pain, which you can choose through your freedom of will and choice.

One of the most powerful uses of energy is through the vibration of the spoken voice. Emotion and thought becomes a word that becomes an action; and all things become possible. The spoken word co-mingles with the soul plan through raised consciousness, and you connect with your Divinity.

The mission of The Angel News Network (TheAngelNewsNetwork.com) is to raise the consciousness, resonance and vibration of the world through teachings and tools received from higher realms, thus allowing spiritual growth and ascension. As you use your energy to intend on creating a new world paradigm of We Consciousness/Unity, you embody the intention of the energy used and create the life you say you want: **communities of equality, harmony and balance.**

You come to see yourselves empowered, supported and guided by the energies you bring into your lives. You first and foremost focus on healing self, allowing the healed me to mirror out into the We. You come to know that your energetic soul is the sum total of all you have experienced, believed, felt, thought and applied through energy.

Finally, you feel and know you are every aspect of *God/Creation/Source/All There Is* experiencing itself, bringing Creation's energy into the world, manifesting a unique vibration that mirrors the divine. Be aware of yourself as divine, and you will connect with the highest energetic vibrations that allow your Divinity to manifest. Consciously reject anything less than the Divine, and it will not exist in your life. You have the power to create the life you say you want -- one of joy, peace, abundance and love. Will you be the best use of your God-given energy? What do you choose?

Alphabetical Listing Of Articles: H

How To Quickly Change Your World
Human Cosmic Construct

How To Quickly Change Your World

From: Archangel Uriel, World Teacher And Guardian.

1. **Redefine** abundance (wealth) through a balance of giving and receiving.

2. **Join** consciousness and joy.

3. **Apply** knowledge into wisdom.

4. **Perform** business through truth, equality and compassion.

5. **Expand** science beyond the human mind.

6. **Practice** religions through spiritual truths (love one another).

7. **Create** governments and politics through unity (we the people, for the people).

Human Cosmic Construct

From: Archangel Uriel, World Teacher And Guardian.

Dear Those Choosing To Be Human,

It is time you know more about your creation and the truth of your existence, which will assist you in moving with grace and ease through your evolutionary Ascension Process (shifting into a higher frequency of reality).

Your Cosmic Construct and evolution is mirrored within the structure of the cosmos. You are now beginning to see yourselves reflected within the cosmos, thus knowing the integration of this truth and wisdom.

The pattern of your solar system planets, initiating with the sun (light) from Mercury to Pluto, reflect the evolution of your species. You began in Light (from the sun) and you are destined to return to Light and begin anew through your freedom of choice and will. This is an eternal, endless process of Creation.

Your being on each of your solar system planets (Mercury, Venus, Earth, Mars, Saturn, Jupiter, Neptune, Uranus and Pluto -- and unknown planets soon to be revealed) are a 'road map' of your evolution as a species. Each planet represents your further awakening. Each planet is a history unto itself to be revealed when you are ready. This has not always been a straight line forward. Each of your evolutionary cycles, on each planet, is a process of growth and expansion and self-mastery preparing you for world and universal service as master teachers. What is unique about the planet you currently reside within and upon is that it is composed of twelve star systems further preparing you for movement further out into the cosmos. Once you finalize your solar system process, you will move into galactic reality, followed by universal and multiversal. Your entire journey is a Light to Light process never ending.

Dear ones, you are realizing there is much to be achieved where you are right now prior to moving on. Having a 'roadmap' is intended to assist you within your current process and journey. The purpose of this message is to reveal the magnificent journey you have chosen being human, and its Divine Design. The entire cosmos has coordinated and is supporting the choice and journey you are making. This is a unique Divine Experiment, 'Lover-versity' of learning, if you will. Once you master the love of self, others, and your world, and create a unity-consciousness reality of equality, harmony and balance, you will be ready to proceed....

Within each evolutionary cycle, you are given a supply of energy to use as you will through your freedom of choice and will. As you may now realize, you have not always used this energy to the best of your highest good or that of others.

Now further knowing and accepting with compassion your joyful journey into service to *All There Is*, we higher realms continue to be in service to the divine cosmic choice you have made. At present, your planet is in the process of clearing and cleansing many issues from the past and present. No matter how things may appear on the outside, please know locked within your DNA is all of which we speak guiding you forward. How and when you get there is your choice. It does not have to be with pain and suffering unless you so choose.

Alphabetical Listing Of Articles: I

I AM: And So Are You!

I AM: And So Are You!

From: Phillip Elton Collins, The Angel News Network.

Inspired By All I've Ever Learned.

I AM breath, sound and motion doing through my being.

I AM God/Source/Creation experiencing all aspects of itself in order to evolve into world service.

I AM activating my Divine Soul Plan (my purpose in being here).

I AM self-empowered through my self-mastery.

I AM not what I have been taught about myself.

I AM an Eternal BEing learning how and what I need to learn to free myself from myself in order to love self, thus others.

I AM density returning to Light.

I AM good enough and worthy enough just the way I am.

I AM not my chronology or just this lifetime.

I AM Love, loving and lovable.

I AM creating communities of equality, harmony and balance.

DIVINE DISCUSSIONS

I AM *that I AM.*

Alphabetical Listing Of Articles: K

Knowing Rather Than Seeking

Knowing Rather Than Seeking

From: Archangel Uriel, World Teacher And Guardian.

Dear Beloved Humans Ascending,

With the current activation of your planet and humanity's Ascension Process, it is time to remember (if you so choose) that your seeking is ending and you are now entering a process of awakening the knowing within your hearts -- to 'think' with your hearts. The portals and vortices networks opening throughout your planet at present are allowing your ability to access the knowing/wisdom within your hearts. Dear ones, the DNA within your hearts contains all the learning from past and present lifetimes. Are you ready to know this is a process of inside out, not outside in? All you need to know is within you, and we higher realms have given you many tools to access this wisdom to assist your individuated soul plan ascension activations. Are you ready to receive them? Love yourselves enough through self-mastery and self-love to access all you need to know and allow the seeking to be a learning tool of the past.

Alphabetical Listing Of Articles: L

Living Parallel Lives

Living Parallel Lives

From: Council of Archangelic Realms (CAR).

Dear Beloved Humans Being Human,

For those of you not familiar with the Council of Archangel Realms (CAR), we are the overseers of the Archangelic Realms who love and support your mission in choosing to be human.

In many of your higher realms teachings from various frequencies, you have heard that you are multi-dimensional beings or are becoming multi-dimensional beings. Many do not completely understand what this means. Allow this to be a brief explanation and expansion of this truth.

Currently, you are experiencing the **third dimension (3D)** through your emotions, thoughts and dense physical bodies. When you sleep or experience physical death, you transition into the **fourth dimension (4D)**, the astral or psychic realm that is a disembodied reflection of your 3D world with no time or space. When you awake from sleep you return to the 3D. You may stay within the 4D for a period of time during physical death. That is necessary to review your past life and prepare yourself for another incarnational cycle to complete lessons from the past life.

When you are ready, you can temporarily advance to the **fifth dimension (5D)** to make decisions with your spiritual guides and personal angels as to what you will choose for your next learning adventure in physical form. Any dimension above 3D is considered a higher realm, since it vibrates at a higher frequency than 3D; the higher the dimension number, the higher the frequency.

All of the above involves being multi-dimensional. Many of you have the ability to experience 3D, 4D and 5D at the same time in a conscious or unconscious state. But there are other aspects to being multi-dimensional that some of you (not all) are also experiencing.

What is about to be said will seem unbelievable for some but will be a known truth for others. This new truth for some begins to explain how extraordinary you truly are as an aspect of Creation (God experiencing itself).

The channel that we are coming through at present (and many others around the planet) experience **"parallel lives" concurrently in multiple locations within higher realm dimensions**. What exactly does this mean? What are some examples you might ask? The first principle is to know that other dimensions exist. The fact that this is not common knowledge applied into wisdom is a core issue for humanity. It is your destiny to know and experience being multi-dimensional as truth. This will be a game changer in your world.

To know there are other dimensions that you experience will shift your religions, governments, corporations, erroneous belief systems and any other elements attempting to control humanity. It will eliminate the few controlling the many.

In addition to Angelic Realms, many other members of the cosmos love and support your planet's soul plan (to learn to love and apply that throughout Creation) and all those within and upon your planet's body. Within the Universal Law of Cause and Effect, what affects one affects all; thus, **some of you have chosen to experience and be in service to multiple lives at the same time.**

There are many Extrastellar Beings (EB's: your brothers and sisters) who wish and intend peace and love for your planet. Some of these advanced beings come from other galaxies and planets and are waiting for the mass of humanity to be able to accept and work with them for the benefit of all. Some of you are sustaining and maintaining conscious and unconscious parallel lives within these higher dimensions.

Many fear contact with EB's from these civilizations, believing they are here to harm or control humanity. While this has taken place within your history, we wish to explain at this time that no harm can come to humanity from **outside** your planet (you have plenty intending harm who are **currently upon** your planet that needs healing). We of the Council of Archangelic Realms, Inner Earth Civilizations, the Galactic Federation and Mother Gaia Earth herself have created and monitor an electronic magnetic force field around the planet that **prevents** any outside harm.

We are here to safeguard the Divine Destiny of this planet since its evolution affects the evolution of *All There Is*. Many universal forces and beings came together to create your world, and you or others will not destroy it. Even if humanity were to destroy itself through your freedom of will and choice, your more conscious planet would evolve into the Being of Light from whence she came. It is your destiny to be and do the same. What do you choose?

There are those of you (such as this channel) who are also having parallel lives with the various advanced

Inner Earth Civilizations who once dwelled upon the surface of this planet. Some of you regularly travel in your Light bodies to the Inner Earth for healing and rest from the chaos of your 3D world.

There can be various conscious, or unconscious, components of you living at the same time in various dimensions all the time. Most of you do not have memory of these events since they can prevent the experience of the now, where you are at present. Each one of your parallel lives (since many of you can have many) are energetically connected to your "Oversoul" (your spiritual entity that has progressed beyond the physical understanding of enlightenment). This allows you to live your various lives in different locations.

The eternally conscious Oversoul keeps up with the various simultaneous lives but does not allow any interference in the various life experiences (soul plans). Since this can be somewhat complicated for your present human mind to understand, let us state it this way:

*If it is your destiny, your Oversoul is facilitating several different lives that occupy different places at the same time. To further clarify, these are **not past lives but present parallel ones**!*

As more of you wake up through the Ascension Process of your planet and humanity, you are destined to become more aware of parallel lives. As we said earlier, this will be an effective game changer for your world. For you and your world to know and apply your expanded knowledge and experiences into your (3D) existence will create the reality of We Consciousness and Oneness. This is a Mighty Mission, indeed!

Now you are beginning to remember and know **all the aspects** of your choice to choose to come to this planet and be human. It is so much more than you ever imagined, or is it? Since you are Creation experiencing itself, we ask you how could it be otherwise?

One of your lives is currently living in a 3D, dualistic, separated, often confronting world, but this is just one of the ways you have chosen to learn 'what is' through 'what is not.'

Can you take non-judging responsibility for the choices you have made to learn here what you need to learn the way you need to learn it?

Through your destined process of permanently moving into a higher frequency of existence, the old way of learning is ending. What you are presently experiencing in your world is a major clearing and cleansing of the old.

Many of your other worldly experiences are bringing in the teachings and tools necessary to move on.

This new truth for many gives new meaning to the phrase, **"You are never alone."**

Alphabetical Listing Of Articles: M

Me Or We, You Choose

Me Or We, You Choose

From: Archangel Uriel, World Teacher And Guardian.

Dear Divine Human Souls,

It is the destiny of your planet and humanity to move from a *'me' consciousness* to a *'We' consciousness*. Let us examine the two forms of consciousness and through your discernment and freedom of will and choice decide what resonates for you. Which do you wish to be?

Me Consciousness

This is a way of feeling and thinking that you are individuals who are only responsible for your own achievements. There is little true intimacy or compassion for or with others. There is little connection to higher realms, from whence you came and love and support you now.

The ways and means to support your human reality/existence are: 1. Materialism/Social Status; 2. Power/Control (few controlling the many); 3. Accumulations of monetary wealth; and 4. Imbalanced focus with the self.

The mental body housing the ego is powered by: 1. Fear; 2. Narcissism/Arrogance; 3, Doubt; 4. Ignorance; 5. Resentment/Rage; and 6. Lack of self-love, thus others.

Most truth is hidden and knowledge and wisdom (applied knowledge) are *replaced* for validation and profit often through deceit and denial of the deceit.

We Consciousness

Through applied knowledge (wisdom) it is understood that you are all connected and integrated and are here to support and love one another in creating communities of equality, harmony and balance.

There is a constant readiness and commitment to support the purpose of each of you being here (soul plan) *through a balance of giving and receiving* and the *balance of the masculine and feminine energies*. There is an innate knowing there is a limitless supply for all.

Truth reigns supreme. There is neither deceit nor denial of the deceit. All information/communication is authentic and transparent. You all know the same thing at the same time.

Heartfelt intentions fill the world, not just ego satisfaction; you are learning to 'think' with your knowing/loving hearts, not just your minds.

The sacred journey of each individual is recognized, honored and valued as an essential aspect of the whole of humanity.

Love is known and seen as the powerhouse of all reality, thus seen in all things -- plants, animals, minerals, air, water and the seen and unseen.

Learning how to heal individual wounds and defenses is mastered, allowing unconditional love, supporting each one's highest good is achieved.

In Conclusion

Which consciousness resonates for you? Once you choose one, fully embrace it in your individual life and radiate it out to others. Be prepared for the responsibilities and consequences of each choice. One of these contains a higher vibration than the other, which will allow the other to entrain to the other. Are you ready to create a new world paradigm? The formula is here, if you so choose to apply it.

Alphabetical Listing Of Articles: N

Nine Necessities: Agreeing To Be Human
No Failure

Nine Necessities: Agreeing To Be Human

From: Archangel Uriel, World Teacher And Guardian.

Dear Beloved Humans,

Within your Ascension Process, it is time to review the agreements you made prior to becoming human. You came from the Light and surely shall return to it.

Your Eternal Spirit Agreed:

1. From Light, you agreed to receive/create a dense carbon-based physical body. The evolution of this body is in the process of transmuting back into Light, soul to spirit. Within this physical body is housed your emotional and mental bodies that complete your humanity. You agreed your emotions and thoughts are creating your reality all the time; that's how powerful you are.

2. This planet is a 'Lover-versity' of learning love. You are learning the necessary lessons/laws of the universe in order to return to Light. You are often learning what is through what is not. Each lifetime and day, within those lifetimes, you are creating and given choices of learning. Some of these lessons may appear harsh, but they are the only way you can learn them in order to free yourselves from your selves. This is preparing you for world and universal service.

3. There are neither accidents nor mistakes within your learning process. Through ownership of each lesson, you shall become free of their cause and effect. Your growth and expansion is not always a straight-line journey.

4. You agreed to repeat all lessons until mastered, until applied knowledge becomes eternal wisdom. When one lesson is learned, you receive the next one; usually core issue lessons for each lifetime.

5. There are lessons to master as long as you reside within a human body. As long as you are within the frequency/dimension you exist within now, your lessons are continuous. When you ascend to a higher frequency this type learning process will not be necessary. Also, remember the universe is an ever-expanding process, as you re-connect to the higher realms that maintain and sustain you.

6. Being present in the now moment will assist you in escaping the entrapment, your agreement of being in the past and future. In reality, now is all there is.

7. Every other person is you in disguise. You agreed not to see the mirror of self in others, but now the end time on that agreement has come.

8. You agreed to accept a supply of energy in each lifetime for you to use through your freedom of will and choice. How you use this energy is up to you; you are evolving to use this energy for the good of all.

9. Everything said here is inside you. You agreed to look outside yourself to seek truth. Now you are realizing all you need to know is inside you and that life is a process of inside out, not outside in. This will allow self-mastery and move you into a higher state of consciousness (ascension).

No Failure

From: Archangel Uriel, World Teacher And Guardian.

In effect, dear ones, there is not failure within your frequency of existence. There are only circumstances you create to learn what you came here to learn and master in order to share it with others, in order to create joyful communities of equality, harmony and balance. If you can accept this truth with compassion and forgive how you have chosen to learn, you will free yourselves from needing to learn the ways of the past and present and create a new future of Divine Love -- the composite of Creation.

Alphabetical Listing Of Articles: O

Only Oneness Omits Isolation
Our Role In Healing

Only Oneness Omits Isolation

From: Cosmic Keepers of Creation.

Dear Humanity Evolving From Duality To Oneness,

With a world filled with separation, duality and often confrontation, perhaps it is time to revisit the reality of Oneness within your existence in order to create a new reality of equality, harmony and balance. How does that feel?

Prior to understanding Oneness, it is essential to understand what creates the opposite of Oneness. It is your life experiences and emotions, which create 'wounds' that then create 'ego defenses,' around the wounds, to defend the wounds. Most of your lives are currently spent *defending* which prevents Oneness. (A deeper study of ego defenses can be gained through many higher realm teachings (one of which is *Activate Your Soul Plan: Angel Answers & Actions*, Chapter 16, by this channel). **Understanding and mastering your defenses is a teaching unto itself and one of the most self-empowering tools available to you.**

Through your freedom of choice and will you have chosen to learn through your wounds and defenses, thus duality and separation. In spite of how things appear in your world at present, it is your destiny to learn another way through Oneness. How and when you achieve this is up to you. When you get sick and tired enough of what you are experiencing, perhaps you will make another choice.

Let us further discuss and 'prove' to your mental body

the reality and benefit of Oneness, with the intent to assist you in moving from your old way of learning to a new, easier paradigm of learning through Oneness. Humanity appears to be addicted to learning the hard way! Why not choose a new way?

One of the most empowering truths within the universe is that of Oneness and how this ancient concept shifts the way humanity perceives and experiences the world. Through the Ascension Process (evolving to a higher consciousness of existence, which the planet and humanity is experiencing at present), it is time to accept with compassion and know that the application of Oneness can and will change humanity, thus the world, for the better and **insure its survival.**

The idea of Oneness is not foreign to humanity. Your religions have moved from duality (many gods) to Oneness reflecting the evolution of humanity. Many religions teach the Oneness of their God and the existence of one all-powerful force in the universe. Metaphysics teaches the Oneness of good and evil, light and dark, right and wrong and male and female (all being aspects of the same Oneness). Universal Law teaches/reveals that Oneness also means that everything, *All There Is*, and all that ever will be, is One; one reality. **In effect, there is nothing in reality that is not Oneness.** Through ascension of the planet and humanity, you are in the personal and collective process of remembering and applying this truth of Oneness. **Oneness is your eternal, divine life insurance policy and pathway to the world you say you want, one of equality harmony and balance.**

Everything in existence is created of the same Oneness 'Cosmic stuff,' atoms, electrons, molecules. These are common qualities that you are exchanging, sharing and replacing all the time. This is the foundation of the Oneness of humanity, as well. Your scientists have proven that all life on the planet is engaged in a great Oneness energetic exchange constantly. Your senses are programmed to see boundaries that often prevent seeing the Oneness. You are, in effect, an individuated aspect of the Whole, the Oneness, whether you see it or are conscious of it or not. You are in the process of waking up and being able to see the truth of your existence.

One of the most hidden aspects of Oneness is the fact that your emotions and thoughts are creating your reality all the time. Emotions and thoughts are components of Oneness, whether they are negative or positive, influencing the Oneness becoming conscious or not. Once your Oneness becomes conscious you create a **unified field of consciousness, which is Oneness.**

Once you fully embrace this unified field of consciousness (Oneness), evolving/ascending further spiritually, you come to know your emotions and thoughts are creating everything (even your weather stored in the atmosphere} as well as assisting the clearing and cleansing of the planet herself. As you become more and more aware of this 'unified Oneness' in action you can begin to take more responsibility for your emotions and thoughts, mastering the **cosmic equation, responsibility=consequence.** When you become responsible you can create consequences more to your liking than the ones you are currently creating (separation from self, others and your world). **Becoming more constructive rather than destructive to the experiences/events in your lives allows the creation of a**

'Oneness environment' that shifts everything into a We Consciousness rather than separation.

Dear ones, can you begin to see that the concept/reality of Oneness allows you to become multidimensional (which you are) and has the ability to recreate a unified new world paradigm to reshape your lives by seeing the interconnectivity of you all and your need to address some new responses (rather than reactions) in your lives and world? You are not just three dimensional aspects (emotions, thoughts and physicality) but are also connected to the unseen world of Oneness, which actually maintains and sustains everything through the Oneness of the Eternal Spirit.

Let us look at it this way: Oneness is all life -- your emotions and thoughts, the Creator, and your physical actions, the manifested result. You are all individuated expressions of Oneness employing the Laws of Cause and Effect and karma, which is the way you have chosen to learn what you need to learn (to learn to love). It is your destiny not to have to learn this way in the future (which is actually now).

Every one of the experiences you create is a personal mirror that invites you to learn more about Oneness, your relationships with self, others, *All There Is*, or reality. **Ultimately, Oneness demands and commands that Oneness is *All There Is*.** You may choose to call Oneness *God*, *Source*, *All There Is*, if any of that resonates for you. Your life experiences are expressions of your Divine Soul Plans (reason to be here) reflecting what you need to learn from lifetime to lifetime. Although you are at present individual, you are One with *All There Is*; **you are One with Oneness.**

DIVINE DISCUSSIONS

Let's create an exercise that further allows you to connect with your Oneness:

For the next week, embrace the concept of seeing the Oneness in everyone with whom you come into contact. Look at each person directly (they do not have to know you are doing this) and feel and think, "I acknowledge the Oneness within each of us." After several days into this exercise, you will notice a shift within yourself as you continue the exercise. Through the integration of the Oneness feelings and thoughts, you will sense a Divine Connection to everyone! You will begin to know that everyone is an aspect/part of you and know you are a part of them. You will realize this is how Oneness (Creation) sees and feels about everything. **You will then know you have individually experienced Oneness.**

Achieving the above shift in consciousness, you become aware that there is more involved in reality than just your mental body or perception. You will begin to **'think' with your heart** and know the purpose of your heart awareness is to allow you to conceive yourself and directly experience yourself to be individuated and yet one with Oneness. In effect, the believing mind is moving back into service to the knowing heart (this is an essential aspect of your evolutionary process).

Through this mind/heart shift the illusion of separation between the observer and the physical world is dissolving: the observer becomes and affects the observed. Quantum physics has proven that observance/energy is a building block of Creation. This energy spreads out infinitely without boundary or set destination. As you move deeper within your knowing heart, you see two realities: one aspect of perception sees the world of separation, while a higher self-perception sees reality as an integrated cosmic choreograph of loving energy. As you continue to 'think' with your heart you come to know what you perceive with your five senses is not the only reality. You come to know what affects one affects the other no matter the time or distance.

Through the concept of Oneness, you are also connecting with the moment of now where there is no time or distance since there is no past or future. **Where there is no time or distance there can be no separation, only Oneness.** Time and distance have been and continue to be the **illusions** that allow you to experience your three dimensional reality of emotions, thoughts, and the physical. Time and distance have been your teaching tools of cause and effect and duality, which are your destiny to end. When and how is up to you in your freedom of choice and will.

Dear ones, your illusions in consciousness and separation were created to provide a laboratory of learning to evolve from the perception of separation to the consciousness of Oneness. You have been learning what is through what is not. This is a tough way to learn but a necessary and effective one based upon your past and present history. All of this is allowing you to know who you are and why you are here and the true meaning, value and purpose of life (to learn to love and serve through that love).

The illusionary outside world that you daily experience and the inner/higher self-world that you identify as being your eternal self are actually one and the same. The outer world is your mirror. The purpose of the reflection in the mirror is to awaken you to your Oneness with *All There Is*. **You are moving from me** consciousness to We Consciousness, Oneness.

In Conclusion

Once you accept with compassion and forgive how you have chosen to learn, you can begin to build communities of equality, harmony and balance in the world: to know that everything is Oneness and everything exists to wake up to this Oneness. All that ever was and is is One. **We are all One.**

Only your Oneness omits your isolation, separation and duality from self, others and your world. When you are ready to embrace the truth of your reality, your Oneness, you will fully reunite with your Divinity, and your service to *All There Is* will be in full force.

Our Role In Healing

From: Akashic Record.

Many standard treatments for illness or disease focus on treating symptoms (with possible side effects) rather than connecting with the core cause and effect of the illness or disease. This discussion is not to judge or shame existing treatments but to gain a deeper understanding of how humanity can innately and naturally create a permanent healing without doing any harm. Perhaps there is a way to create comprehensive /integrated medicine that uses existing and alternative approaches. **The goal is to involve the patient while doing no harm and create a lasting healing.**

What is missing, not understood, or believed, in standard medicine are the unseen forces that create life -- energetic/spiritual components that maintain and sustain life. Humanity has learned a lot about the physical structures and functions of the human body; now humanity needs to master what actually allows it to live in combination with what is currently known. This will require the 'knowing mind' to surrender to not knowing and allow wisdom beyond the mind to come forth. **The energetic/spiritual is the 'God Power' of life, emotions and thoughts the contractor and the physical body the end result.**

What humanity intends to do now is combine the energetic/spiritual, emotional, mental and the physical as aspects of the whole human being in creating a holistic approach to healing. In the recent past and present humanity focused mainly on the physical while maintaining disease without sustaining a majority of permanent healings. Maintaining disease, rather than healing, has become big business with little monetary incentive to find cures. As consciousness increases (which is humanity's destiny) the 'greed-factor' in medicine will decrease and eventually be eliminated as humanity evolves into true healing.

Another key element missing within many approaches to medicine and healing is self-empowerment through the proactive and often preventive involvement of the patient. True healing is a process of inside out, not outside in. Most of standard medicine approaches involve outside in approaches: take this pill, have this surgery, do this therapy. This is not to say these cannot sometimes (temporarily?) improve the situation but often at a consequence that may create something that was not present initially. How much actual permanent healing is taking place? is the question.

Involving the patient in the process of their own healing, often beginning by allowing them to be heard is vital! Healing begins with nurturing first by allowing the patient to explain in detail exactly what the problem is and why they desire to heal it. This begins the balancing of the energetic/spiritual life forces flowing through humanity and focuses on the desire to harness this force for healing. This also begins the process of allowing the emotional and mental bodies to communicate with the physical body (knowing that all physical imbalances begin with the emotions and their created thoughts).

The involvement of energy flow, its balance or imbalance within the physical body and the effect of emotions on this energy flow are the major missing wisdom in medicine today. This discussion is to be a template and basic outline for a holistic medical approach. For a complete study of energy and emotions within the human body, please refer to The Angel News Network publications: *Activate Your Soul Plan!: Angel Answers & Actions*, by this author, Chapter 48 "What is Life & The True Cure For Disease." This is an adapted teaching from Archangel Gabriel originally published in *The Second Coming, Archangel Gabriel Proclaims A New Age*, by Joel D. Anastasi.

As humanity further awakens within its consciousness, it is essential to know that **disease is not a punishment or a test to be endured through long suffering but a learning tool to further awaken humanity's purpose for healing by knowing their purpose for living**. These purposes can be revealed by knowing who you are (spiritual beings having a human experience) and why you are here (to learn to love self, thus others and the world). Why you want to get well, to heal, is the spiritual/energetic force within the healing process. Activating/evoking purpose, in this way, places healing in a much larger energetic arena than simply addressing a physical problem/symptom. Knowing the 'who' and 'why' of your lives assists in manifesting the healing through your reason to be here.

As in all matters of life, seeing the positive/teaching within an illness situation allows humans to take ownership, release victimhood and find the meaning, value and purpose that is the pathway to the healing process. Much of humanity knows stories about how people's lives changed and took an unknown positive path because of a disease. The forces that created humanity are not here to punish but to love and support humanity through whatever means are necessary to learn what humanity needs to learn the way humanity needs to learn it. **This allows humanity to know they are co-creators with Creation, as they assume responsibility for being the self-empowered master of their own healing.** This does not mean that humans cannot ask for the support of others.

The human mind is still asking why there are diseases and a need for healing. Another way to explain is that humanity has not so simply stepped off the path of its true Divinity, its direct connection to *All There Is*. **Everything discussed here is about resetting humanity's soul plan compass.** Quite simply, humanity has imbalanced their lives and world, and now physical bodies are mirroring/reflecting one another, communicating that problem to humanity. Since the world and humanity are made of the same Cosmic stuff, it is only natural that their 'talking bodies' are trying to wake humanity up and effect change.

Finally, let us review and suggest four other steps to assist in healing:

For healing to occur, **the first step** is to know something is wrong. You don't feel well. What is it? Since healing is a process of inside out, it is essential that you move inward with an attitude of gratitude that begins to reveal the healing. **True healing begins with consciousness/awareness.**

A **second step** would be to accept with compassion thus forgive what you have created in order to learn what you need to learn the way you need to learn it. True healing/transformation requires accepting all aspects of yourself (a deep examination of the self) that has been unknown/unconscious, moving into your present awareness: this is a vital component of healing. There is a self-mastery (personal processing) program entitled *Life Mastery, A Guide For Creating The Life You Want And The Courage To Live It*. This is a teaching from Archangel Michael via trance channel Jeff Fasano, workshop created by Joel D. Anastasi that we may suggest, if you so choose.

As you accept with compassion and forgive the experience you create, you can personally process more of the previously unfelt/unaccepted feelings allowing the energetic/spiritual access for healing. Then you become more emotionally and physically balanced allowing true healing.

The **third step** is to know **you are the major player in the inside out healing process.** Once you release any judgment or shaming of what you have created, you can better allow an assessment of what the next best steps are through your resonance (how you feel about it) and your discernment (how you think about it). Each human is responsible for the **'common sense' matters of health** such as diet and exercise, honoring the body temple that houses your emotions and thoughts. Then the unseen aspects of self come into play such as the discussed emotions, attitudes, spiritual beliefs, and any confirmed therapies you have decided upon. Previously, we discussed the importance of being heard that can be very healing/therapeutic. This can be done with your own diary and certainly speaking and being heard with your health-care people. Since you are composed of energy, raising the vibrations within the body is vital. **There is no better way to do this than through joy.** Find people and activities that allow you to laugh at your 'condition' knowing you are not your disease. Play in nature and look in the mirror everyday knowing you came from Love, you are Love, and you are lovable and loved.

The final **forth step** is to **remember your emotions and thoughts create your reality**. Also, check in with your belief systems. If some erroneous beliefs become your knowing, that is what you will experience. This is how powerful you are. You are teaching your body to entrain to the highest vibration, thus balance its energy flow and heal. You are learning to employ 'energy medicine', and the vital role of the unseen forces in bringing about the healing of the physical. There are breathing techniques, meditations, and energy exercises that abound in the world to assist you.

In Conclusion

All of what humanity creates is meant for humanity to know itself and better understand the ways it creates. **Any health situation is a way to wake up through healing.** When humanity is not just trying to fix or get rid of a health issue, but see it as a learning tool (not a punishment), it can become a transformation of individual lives and humanity. That is the healing.

Alphabetical Listing Of Articles: R

Religions And Christ Consciousness
Rest In Peace 3-D
Resurrection: Christ Consciousness
(Transcending All Beliefs Into Cosmic Truth)

DIVINE DISCUSSIONS

Religions And Christ Consciousness

From: Phillip Elton Collins, The Angel News Network.

There have been more wars and killing in the name of religions and their founding figures than any other force on Earth. Today we continue to see extreme, distorted examples of this. We have taken our religions that are filled with spiritual truths (love one another) and used them as an abrupt example of duality, separation and confrontation. This does not mean that many religions have not done and continue to do good work. They do. **But the time has come for our religions to transcend into communities of equality, harmony and balance through We Consciousness/Unity; moving from the wounded me to the healed We, controlling no one in equality.** All the founding figures of **religions** shared at their core universal truths through something called Christ Consciousness, which is about connecting humanity to our Divinity, not through any one religion. We all have some form of attachment to the word 'Christ' be it positive or negative. **It is time, if we so choose, to better understand this 'Christ Consciousness,' its meaning, value and purpose beyond and including all organized religions.**

God's Glossary: A Divine Dictionary defines *Christ Consciousness as the reality and connection to your Divine Essence; there have been many embodiments and messengers of this teaching throughout human history; it lives within each of you waiting to be awakened.*

Realizing that words can get in the way, this force,

consciousness, state of being, called Christ Consciousness has been on this planet ever since its creation. It is a band of consciousness to unite us not separate us, which mankind has attempted to do with it. Let us further examine this Divine Energy called 'Christ Consciousness' with the intention to bring us closer together while supporting whatever religious or spiritual beliefs individuals need to embrace. It is essential as a species that we support each other's freedom of choice and will while speaking truth.

The Christ Consciousness is not about any one religion; it is about the essence of humanity and our united Divine Destiny and destination to be God experiencing itself. All of our many lifetimes on this planet have been to know our connection of Oneness to one another and Creation, call it *God/Source/All There Is*. The Christ Consciousness energy, many times incarnated in religious founding figures throughout our Earth history, is a pathway back to our Divinity for each and every one of us.

Throughout our often mistranslated and intentionally biased history and personal experiences, the word 'Christ' has received many definitions and terrible things done in the name of it that do not reflect the true meaning of Christ Consciousness. (The initial response to the name Christ for most Christians is 'positive,' for most non-Christians the response is negative). Many religious figures and founders have received the Christ Consciousness energy within themselves through various means and given those teachings to the world. The word 'Christ' is a union and Oneness with Creation/God; 'Christ Consciousness' is a way showing to that union. We might say man power becoming God

Power. Whoever the individual or the religion or other spiritual path, the consciousness is about reuniting with the Divine and returning to a state of Oneness.

This story of reuniting with the Divine has been told many ways through many religions throughout our Earth history. We were once connected to the Divine and through various human activities separated from that Truth. Our 'human contract' and journey via our freedom of choice and will was not always in accord with Universal Laws and Truth. This was and is the way we chose to learn what we needed to learn the way we needed to learn it (through separation, duality and confrontation), a tough way to learn but an effective one! We are beginning to wake up in our world today, in spite of continued upheavals, to our true BEingness and destiny to Oneness. At some point we shall completely wake up, make the choice to return from whence we came and experience self-mastery and devotion to world service. It's just a matter of how and when for each of us.

The personal process in consciousness is a self-mastery or a self-empowerment, self-realization, leading to life mastery, connecting the higher self (the Christ self), allowing the self to be fully realized through its Divine Essence.

Rather than being a messenger restricted or exclusive to any one religion, Christ Consciousness embodies a universal truth of self for all of humanity. So no matter what religion you choose or your personal belief systems, the 'Christ energy' exists in possibility and probability for all of humanity.

Seeing Christ Consciousness as a template for humanity

is helpful, like an older brother or sister who, had been there before and is lending a helping hand, a loving hand showing us the way back home: A cosmic living sibling combining Earth and spirit showing us that each one of us also shares the same relationship with God/Creation. We are all ultimately 'Children of Creation' made of Cosmic stuff, learning that one child's needs are no different from the others. We are all evolving into becoming a (human) being reflecting the Divinity within Christ Consciousness itself, **the real second coming.**

We humans are not only 'Children of Creation', we are Divine Destiny becoming 'gods-in-the-making', since everyone is an aspect of Creation/God finally realizing that everything in the universe is integrated.

Discovering cosmic Christ Consciousness witnessed throughout our human history (Lemuria, Atlantis, Egypt, Greece, Roman, Mayan, Aztec, Hopi, etc.) allows us to know the Divine-Consciousness within each and every one of us. This consciousness has little to do with our religions per se and everything to do/be with the individual's soul growth and expansion. This cosmic Christ Consciousness reflects a living cosmos **filled with presence** that knows the soul of mankind is immortal. We come to know that the universe is balanced by bands of a Loving Consciousness, which is the foundation of Creation.

Christ Consciousness is filled with the energies of love, forgiveness, compassion, acceptance, patience and Oneness, allowing the individual to move into caring for others through self-love, thus generating world service. In effect, we become *companions with Creation,* reflecting our evolutionary soul plan activation of knowing we came from Love, are Love and are loved and lovable. Love as the building block allows us to construct a new Earth paradigm of We Consciousness/Oneness.

Creation's way to download consciousness to humanity is through Christ Consciousness in which life experiences itself in a continuous personal processing of awakening. We are entering an ascension epoch (moving to a higher frequency of existence) where humanity experiences the complete total of their individual consciousness moving into wholeness: to know thy self.

Another purpose of Christ Consciousness is that it allows the universe to be observed, allowing Creation to become conscious of itself through evolution. Humanity knows it is here and can ask the questions, where do we come from? Why are we here? Who are we? (No other life form on this planet does this or has this need). Christ Consciousness has within it an energetic blueprint that will answer these eternal questions, containing universal wisdoms within the foundation of most religions.

Christ Consciousness teaches us that all truth inevitably comes from the same cosmic Source. Truth is stored within the DNA of your knowing heart from lifetime to lifetime, allowing the believing mind to move back into service to the knowing heart. We, in effect, are now learning to 'think' with our hearts. In reality, each of us chooses from lifetime to lifetime the best learning experiences/tools we need to learn what we need to learn the way we need to learn it.

Our Christ Consciousness is our light worker and way shower within, a gift from the gods, the very best aspect of self, all loving and forgiving while nurturing the wounded me moving into the healed We, finally arriving at our divine destination: our united Divinity.

God's Glossary: A Divine Dictionary defines **Divinity** *as your connection to your soul; Oneness; achieving higher consciousness; true self; Christ Self as One; God Consciousness; spiritual causation balancing non-perfection.*

DIVINE DISCUSSIONS

Rest In Peace 3-D

From: Archangel Uriel, World Teacher And Guardian.

As an essential aspect of being human, *the human contract agreement*, and due to humanity's separation from the higher realms who maintain and sustain humanity (thinking they could do it a better way), for eons humans have been **learning what is through what is not** through duality and separation often leading to confrontation.

Through the Ascension Process of planet Earth (moving into a higher frequency of existence), humanity is beginning to evolve beyond emotional, mental and physical components of the third dimension (3D) of which they presently reside. What you see in the world today is the necessary clearing and cleansing in order for humanity to evolve. Things may look worse, but it is actually the darkness before the dawn.

Humanity is beginning to realize they have had enough of **polarity consciousness** and are ready to commit to building communities of equality, harmony and balance through We Consciousness by reconnecting to the higher fifth dimensional energies who maintain and sustain humanity's existence.

By also balancing human energies with that of humanity's ascending planet (moving from dense carbon to the Light from whence humanity came), humanity shall finally recreate the final golden age of their home planet. Then humanity shall recreate the paradise this beautiful planet was intended to be and not have to lose it again.

Then the third dimension can become a loving memory (rest in peace) from which humanity no longer needs to learn. Are you ready? I am!

Resurrection: Christ Consciousness Energy (Transcending All Beliefs Into Cosmic Truth)

From: Phillip Elton Collins, The Angel News Network.

Beloved Fellow Humans,

In large part, erroneous belief systems support the idea that the Jesus Christ resurrection was something only He could achieve. That it was some kind of high and mighty miracle only achievable by a higher power through a certain religion. As a result of accepting this as truth, humanity is experiencing lack and limitation and so called death as a natural aspect of life. **One of the most important reasons Christ (meaning soul) experienced the resurrection was to maintain and sustain an energetic pathway within our consciousness, that all of humanity is capable of employing each and every day.**

This resurrection gift and energy is the promise to humanity of our transcending what we have been experiencing as lack, limitation, and separation, evolving back into our Divinity. The resurrection energy is being activated within our spiritual DNA and expanding chakra system ever more quickly during our Easter Season when Mother Earth takes a massive **out-breath** creating Spring and **rebirth of *All There Is*.** Winter is the **in-breath** of the planet. This is how our planet breathes and maintains and sustains our life upon and within her body.

Resurrection means to return to a normal state of being by transitioning wounds and ego defenses to higher

realms. Who we are is not only God being BEingness, but also God being we as co-creators. This truth brings resurrection out of the miraculous into a universal law, and availability, in which we can heal and restore all imbalances into wholeness and Oneness. **Seeing so-called death transmuting into life is the normal state of every divine soul. True resurrection transcends any one belief or organization that attempts to take ownership of something they did not create.**

If a plant that has been dormant all Winter can come to life again through the resurrection energy from within the core of the Earth at Spring Season, why not us? This resurrection energy is actually available all the time, a limitless free supply (for us to see ourselves worthy enough) to invoke and apply.

Take a deep breath and allow yourself especially at Easter Season to feel the resurrection energy awaken within you. Invoke this birthright empowerment until you can actually feel and know it. Connect with your higher self, I AM Presence, and allow your affirmation to be, "*I AM the Resurrection and the Life.*" With these simple yet powerful universal few words, you can build/employ this resurrection energy within and throughout whatever needs to be healed and released from your emotional, mental and physical bodies, thus world. These divinely inspired words allow us all to resurrect ourselves from any and all crucifixions (learning to love self and others).

Repeat several times out loud, "*I AM the Resurrection and The Life*," and follow these 'coded' words with whatever needs to be healed and released from your life. Allow yourself to accept with compassion and gratitude the Divine Gift of resurrection.

Our divine birthright of always being able to resurrect ourselves back into our Divinity will be the eventual pathway to returning to our eternal, immortal state of BEing.

Are you ready to resurrect and release whatever is necessary in order to return to your Divinity? **This is the true Christ's (meaning soul's)** *second coming;* **a process of inside out, not outside in.**

Our ascending world awaits the resurrection of all human wounds and ego defenses into Oneness.

Everlasting Easter Season Resurrection Energy to One and All!

Alphabetical Listing Of Articles: S

Sacred Trilogy Of Teachings
*Sacred Trilogy Of Teachings
*Seven Sacred Flames: How To Use Them
*Seven Sacred Flames: Daily Use
*Sacred Shifts To Ascend
*Seven Sacred Steps For Your Ascension
*Seven Sacred Flames Chart

§

Seven Aspects Of Ascension
Saint Francis Energy
Separating From Separation Into Oneness
Some Ways To Love More
Spirituality And/Or Religion
Summer Solstice Letter

Sacred Trilogy Of Teachings

The *Seven Sacred Flames*, *Sacred Shifts* and *Sacred Steps* teachings have been presented to humanity in many past ages (Lemuria, Atlantis, early Egypt, Aztec, Mayan civilizations and others) by higher realms such as the Archangelic Realms, Inner Earth Civilizations, the Ascended Masters and many more. These teachings are a gift to humanity to free ourselves from ourselves.

This trilogy of teachings offers concise, easily understood wisdoms to explain the significance of the current planetary vortices and portals that are activated across our planet now. These planetary activations offer powerful support to the ascension of our planet and of humanity in which we will return to the Light by embracing our Divinity.

This body of teachings comes from Adama, the Father of Humanity and High Priest of Telos, Lemuria, Inner Earth Civilization. For those not familiar with Adama or Lemuria, you have a wonderful journey of discovery ahead of you, if you choose. Read these words of wisdom and see if they resonate within your hearts and within the discernment of your minds. This teaching (pages 168-192) is also available with audios via PhillipEltonCollins.com.

The Light of Source Never Fails.

Seven Sacred Flames: How To Use Them

From: Adama, Father of Humanity, High Priest of Telos, Lemuria, Inner Earth Civilization.

Beloved Humanity (God Being Man),

Upon the surface of this laboratory of learning love (planet Earth), we of the energies and consciousness of the Inner Earth Civilization of Lemuria, at this crucial time within your Ascension Process (raising your frequency to advance in order to join us), once again offer daily tools to assist your process and journey to return to your Divinity. There were those of you who believed that your ascension would automatically take place during 2012. At this time, we wish to review and introduce to you the purpose and continued gift of the *Seven Sacred Flames* and how to apply them within your weekly calendar. Ascension is an individuated process of inside out, not outside in. You are all destined to arrive at your ascension. You are all in the process of ascending. How and when you arrive is your freedom of choice and will.

We within the Inner Earth Civilization of Lemuria, who once dwelled upon the surface of this planet like you now do, have held in daily devotion our love and support for these *Seven Sacred Flames* for eons. These have allowed a frequency and pathway for you upon the surface to journey back Home to your Divinity and not repeat the insanity of the past. It is time, if you so choose, to begin supporting these flames in a daily more forthright way. The reason we went from the surface of the planet to the interior (receiving a dispensation from higher realms) was due to the wars and abuse of the planet, not unlike what you are experiencing now, but in a more advanced, extreme way.

The correlation of these *Seven Sacred Flames* to your soul plans, chakra system and days of the week is another demonstration of the perfected design of the universe and you. This is a more simplified, concise presentation of this teaching than ever before. The intention of this simplified teaching is to allow a faster integration of these energies during these times of transition.

What Are The *Seven Sacred Flames*?

The *Seven Sacred Flames* are bands of energy and consciousness from Creation to support the Divine Soul Plan of this planet and all things within and upon it; this includes you! The purpose of this planet is to express Love by learning to love (the building block of Creation) self, your purpose/endeavor in being here, others, and to be in service to your world. You came from Love; you are Love and lovable. The *Seven Sacred Flames* are gifted to your planet every day of the seven days of the week. Each day has a correlation flame that also connects to your seven chakras system (which reflects the star systems that seeded your planet), which maintains and sustains your existence upon the planet. Becoming aware/conscious of each flame and its respective day will assist you in maintaining the balance of your emotional, mental and physical bodies, thus advancing your ascension. How you feel and think affects your energy flow and balance and creates your reality each day. Within your Ascension Process, it is essential to balance and consciously apply these sacred flames to further embrace your Divine Destiny to return to being the Eternal BEings Of Light you are. For those of you receiving this wisdom and truth at this time, it is an important fragment of your soul plan, if you so choose, that you do so.

What Do The Names Of The Days Really Mean?

Your present days of the week were named by the Romans using Latin words; the English versions reflect an Anglo-Saxon influence of gods and mythological figures. Each day of the week is also affected by the electromagnetic force field inside and around the planet, since each day is positioned within a different 3D Earth time. **What has been lost and/or confused is that the names of the days of your week are also the planetary ascension pathway/journey of humanity within this solar system:** (This is a vast teaching unto itself, which will soon be revealed to humanity when you are ready to know and accept your origins and true history.) Beginning with the Sun for Sunday (the birth mother of the planets), followed by Monday for the Moon where much of the DNA for humanity was originally stored, Tuesday for Mars, Wednesday for Mercury, Thursday for Jupiter, Friday for Venus and Saturday for Saturn. Through your distorted history, the actual order of the planets within the solar system and the day names within the week have been misaligned. Suffice to say, the names of the days, your chakras and these *Seven Sacred Flames* all have Divine meaning, value and purpose and are interrelated, as all things within the universe are!

What Is The Chakra System?

Many of you are familiar with the name and/or function of your chakras system. Each of these seven major chakras are primary energy centers that has its own character and corresponds to a unique aspect of your being. You are in the Ascension Process of activating an additional five chakra systems to complete the connection to the twelve star systems that seeded your planet. From the first chakra (physical vitality or survival) to the seventh chakra (totality of BEingness or spiritual perfection), the chakras are spiritual/energetic entities, each a realm of being and consciousness. The energetic functions within each chakra are what make every aspect of your bodily, emotional, mental and spiritual life possible. Every chakra is receiving energy into itself from all around and this energy supports the energy field and the entire life process of you. **We shall now correlate each chakra with a specific Sacred Flame and day of the week to further support your Ascension Process. Please notice there are seven flames, seven chakras and seven days divinely designed to work together. The number seven contains an energetic 3D density building block upload and foundation for life as you know it.**

The Flame Of The Will Of God

Day: Monday, First Day Of Week And Initial Flame Needed

Chakra: Throat-- Creative Expression, Expressive Communication, Self-Empowerment, Telepathy

God is Love and God's love is unconditional. What humanity is at present learning is to love self, others and your endeavors in order to be in world service. This **Will Of God** being Love is the attribute that will facilitate your Ascension Process, and it is an important way to begin your week, focusing on this truth. A good way to begin is by having gratitude for what is in your life rather than focusing on what is not. Surrender to what is, let go of your fears (absence of Love), judgments and shaming of self and others through love. You can best be in world service by clearing and cleansing yourself first. See everything you create in your life (and you are creating it all) as a learning tool by taking ownership of it all. Accept with compassion and forgive how you have chosen to learn what you need to learn the way you need to finally learn it. The universe would be incomplete without each and every one of you (or you would not be here) and is divinely designed to give you exactly what you need (only you are preventing that through your relationship with self). How long have you mistrusted or not remembered or known the forces (God) that created you? Surrendering to God's Will (this flame) of Love allows you to finally embrace your divine birthright. Perhaps you not trusting you being God is what needs to heal now. It is time, if you so choose, to let go of the fears that gave birth to this lack of trust that has been passed on for many incarnational cycles. In effect, trusting God is also allowing the commitment to your Higher Self/Soul Plan that you intend to achieve ascension through self-mastery.

The Flame Of Cosmic Love

Day: Tuesday

Chakra: Heart-- Acceptance, Compassion, Empathy, Forgiveness, Unconditional Love

Building upon the previous Flame, the love of God, you being God, experiencing itself, this Tuesday Flame's energy is about a deeper, true understanding and meaning of Love. This Flame eternally lives within your heart signifying to the universe that you are a Divine

BEing having a human experience, knowing that you are God experiencing itself in *All Ways*. Through the Love directed through this heart flame, you come to know you are a student at the 'Lover-versity', Planet Earth, to become Love incarnate by creating communities of equality, harmony and balance. Divine Love is changeless and constant and not dependent upon anyone or anything. It is the highest vibrational building block of Creation. Love within this Cosmic Love Flame is the highest expression of Creation and it is your destiny to become your highest expression of self. Cosmic Love is a neutral and organic expression and activity of God/Creation; human love is a mere distorted reflection of this love. Cosmic Love is not a human feeling being emoted; it is the Law of Attraction in action that attracts like kind. This Love Flame contains acceptance, compassion and forgiveness to free you from yourself. It is an energy that creates miracles, heals emotional, mental and physical imbalances and connects you to the higher realms from whence it and you originated. Cosmic Love is the only true and lasting force in all Creation; it is the power and vibration of life. It is you becoming you! Call upon this Flame at the beginning of your Tuesday and see what terrific Tuesdays you tote.

Flame Of Healing And Manifestation

Day: Wednesday

Chakra: Third Eye (Forehead)-- Higher Realm Sight, Precognitive Dreams, Inspiration, Visualization

This Sacred Flame's energy is about a process of healing from the inside out. Anytime you assist your or another's healing it is a process of your receiving and allowing the giving and receiving to self or another to heal themselves. Unfortunately, most of humanity does not know the cause and effect of the energetic imbalances, which create what you call dis-ease and death (death being the final hurdle for humanity to free itself). Most of your dis-eases and imbalances are caused by an imbalance of energy flows throughout the body. (The complete science of this is available to you through the Archangelic Realms serving humanity through this endeavor called The Angel News Network). The emotional body creates these imbalances. During the present Ascension Process of the planet and humanity, the accumulation of emotional trauma from past and present life times is taking place. What is taking place now is a final clearing and healing. To truly heal the physical body, you need to first heal/feel/release the deep-seated feelings that cause the imbalance (not being worthy or good enough). When balance and harmony are regained, the body will automatically balance and the healing can become permanent. There are personal processing tools available to you from higher realms to assist you. Ask and you will receive. You are designed and created to be in a perfect state of health; your higher selves can never be ill. You are not your illness. What you create in your bodies is not so simply a way you have chosen to learn what it is you need to learn the way you need to learn it. Because of the misuse and abuse of your freedom of choice and will, and lack of self-mastery and applied love due to uncontrolled emotions and thoughts, you have created the reality that exists in your personal lives and world. Internal and external pains are always mirrors of inner pains and fears. These mirror what needs to heal and transmute through your consciousness. If you so choose, it is now time to thoroughly heal the past and present, embrace and create a new paradigm of We

Consciousness/Unity based upon Love for yourselves, one another, your soul plan and planet. There are many higher realm tools and messages available to you to achieve all of which we speak. Are you ready to apply them?

Flame Of Resurrection

Day: Thursday

Chakra: Solar Plexus-- Creation Of Self, Perception, Self-Empowerment, Understanding the emotional body in relationship to the mental and physical bodies

This Thursday Flame focuses on the energies for the resurrection and self-empowerment of your destined Divinity. You have chosen as a Divine BEing to have the human experience to learn what you agreed to learn the way you are learning it. The reason you have chosen this path is to become the master teachers of your world and beyond. Straying from consciousness into duality and separation has veiled you from your truth, but connecting with this Flame's energy will reconnect you. Remember, freeing you from yourselves through ascension is the main reason for your many lifetimes on this Earth. Through the balancing of the masculine and feminine energies, you will further come to know who you are and why you are here, while discovering and applying your gifts and talents into We Consciousness. In fact, you are within the final epoch of your planet, creating the long awaited final Golden Age of moving from the shadows to the light. Again, we wish to remind you there are many teachings and tools from we higher realms to assist you. The time is upon you to awaken and remove the man-made dogmas and doctrines which have kept you prisoner on your own planet too long.

This Flame has the power of resurrection for all of humanity, raising the vibration of the planet for all within and upon it while transmuting all density into Light. You came from Light. You will return to Light. Where there is Light there can be no lack and limitation. Your self-love mirroring out into the world powers the Resurrection Flame. Your self-love allows you to receive and give in balance knowing you are Creators through feelings of gratitude. Knowing and loving your higher, Divine Self will create the life you say you want. It is time, if you choose, to cast out all fear, doubt and ignorance (the monsters of humanity) and surrender to not knowing in order to allow all Divine possibilities and probabilities to arise. When you live in the moment of now, you live with the Resurrection Flame, which holds the blueprint of your Divine Soul Plan (your purpose in being here). Many of you believe (from the mind) and some know (from the heart) that your ascension is possible. But the mind wants to know how and when. The process of self-mastery is a unique process for each one of you that will be revealed the moment it is meant to be. Through your BEingness, you, the Creator, will create.

The Ascension Flame

Day: Friday

Chakra: Sacral-- Desire (including sexual energy), Intuition, Self-Reliance

Ascension is a Divine Process of the transmuting of your dense (carbon based) human self into your Light-bodied etheric higher self-- moving from unhealed me consciousness into united We Consciousness. During this process, all negative emotions and thoughts, false beliefs, habits and patterns that no longer support your highest good and ascension are dissolved. The Ascension Flame is an energetic, essential tool to assist your journey. During the Ascension Process, it is necessary to learn to control and transmute any and all emotions and thoughts that do not reflect your higher self. Many Universal Laws such as Cause and Effect, Balance of Giving and Receiving, Balance of Masculine and Feminine Energies and Karmic Consequence have been gifted to humanity to speed your Ascension Process. The Universe is balanced through such laws, and it is your destiny to know and master them. The Ascension Flame also holds the energies of unconditional love, balance and harmony that allow the creation of communities of equality, harmony and balance. All life forms need to be respected and honored in order to live together in peace knowing you are all essential aspects of this planet. Connecting directly to the higher realms that maintain and sustain your existence and becoming multi-dimensional is the new normal. Honoring the body temple that houses your emotions, thoughts and physical being will allow the transmuting of that body into Light at the appropriate moment for each of you. Through the Ascension Flame every atom, electron, and cell of your body transmutes completely into your ascended mastership to be in world service and beyond. Since the planet (a conscious being) herself has chosen to ascend into Light (become a star) all upon and within her body will transform to Light as well. This is the destiny of all planets born from Light to return to it. Those who choose not to ascend will be given an opportunity elsewhere. It is a time to surrender with joy and an attitude of gratitude for the amazing opportunity being gifted to humanity, if you so choose. As your world continues to appear in upheaval, perhaps it is time to release your old patterns of behavior and accept with compassion your true BEingness of love. Your planet is going to ascend with or without you. What do you choose? Know through your heart that your past and present behavior will not be tolerated much longer, and your lack of consciousness will heal. It is up to you when and how.

The Violet Flame Of Transmutation

Day: Saturday

Chakra: Root (Base Of Spine, Seat Of The Soul)-- Physical Vitality, Sexuality, Survival Instinct

If it resonates on Saturday (when this Flame is most powerful) connect with the vibrations of the Violet Flame, which induces the frequency of shifts/change, freedom from self's lack and limitations, initiating the clearing and cleansing of wounds and ego defenses, which prevent your self-mastery. This Flame is very effective in balancing the emotional and mental bodies, which can contain negative emotions and thoughts affecting your reality. Being present in the now moments of life (through the Violet Flame) clears many aspects of the past and future (affecting the now). Accepting with compassion your Divinity and your pathway to it are essential aspects of this Flame. Your resistance to who you truly are is reduced greatly in the presence of this tool. The balanced energies of the divine masculine and divine feminine affects positive, permanent change and can dissolve karma through this violet frequency. Universal Law requires resolution to all matters through acceptance and compassion, thus forgiveness (key ingredients within this Flame). Intending no hidden personal or political agenda through this energy can and will produce peace on Earth. This planet can no longer tolerate the continued abuse of humanity and survive. The new world Unity paradigm for Earth and your selected leaders will largely come from violet frequencies. People will become more aware of how they are creating the world you see now and can begin to make another choice. It is essential that people become conscious of their emotions/thoughts that create actions. Your weather patterns are created by the stored emotions and thoughts within your atmosphere and radiate out into the cosmos. The Violet Flame can allow the learning of needed lessons through grace and ease rather than through destruction and pain.

The Illumination & Wisdom Flame

Day: Sunday

Chakra: Crown– Enlightenment/Spiritual Perfection, Totality Of BEingness, Undifferentiated Consciousness

This Flame focuses on the Divine Mind (Mind of God) which can reflect into your own human mental body and allow the believing human mind to return in service to the knowing heart. Truth and applied knowledge (wisdom) and consciousness lives within this Divine Mind. As you learn to connect with this higher mind, you can surely create and illuminate the life and world you say you want. This Sunday Flame increases not only illumination, through wisdom, but supports your bringing your talents and gifts out into the world in order to raise the vibration and frequency of humanity. Through your resonance, discernment and teaching truth (there is very little Truth in your world today) you enlighten your world. This Flame further allows humanity to know exactly what is going on in the world, revealing the hidden forces that have been controlling your planet for eons. More than ever, humanity is in need of consciousness and enlightenment to fully understand and accept your Divinity, in contrast to what is transpiring in your world at present. Humanity has been asleep for a long time and much separation, confrontation and pain have been created as a result of your slumber. Incarnation after incarnation you have brought the erroneous imprints from past lives into the present. The time has come for this to stop and to see your Divinity in full focus. Your true nature as a spiritual being is a state of BEing, an awakened state of consciousness that brings you back to the reality of you being Love, loved and lovable -- allowing your Divinity to express fully through your BEingness reflected in your doingness. This Flame represents man power transmuting into God Power, wisdom (applied knowledge) into any and all areas needed in your life. The Mind of God represents a Cosmic Consciousness that knows all without limitation; the human mind is fettered by the ego filled with wounds and defenses, untrue beliefs about self, others and your world. What is needed and supplied here is a transformation through applied knowledge (wisdom), allowing the release of patterns and habits that no longer serve you or your world. If you are willing to be and do the work, (all tools are available to you) you can transform yourself and your world into the paradise that exists in higher realms. This is the human contract you signed and agreed to before coming here. It is all your choice. No one can nor will force you into embracing your Divinity. Your evolution is assured. How and when you arrive is up to you through your freedom of choice and will.

Conclusion

These *Seven Sacred Flames* are essential aspects of your Ascension Process enrolled at the 'Lover-versity', called planet Earth. It is time for humanity to bring its own personal contribution and use of these Sacred Flames into your daily lives, if you so choose. The Inner Earth Civilizations have maintained and sustained these flames for eons so you have a path Home. It is time for you to take responsibility for these truths and tools yourselves to prevent a consequence not fully to your liking.

The daily use of these Flames creates an energetic upload to support your personal Ascension Process. The teachings within these Flames contain cosmic truths to awaken humanity from a deep sleep. These Sacred Frequency Flames contain Divine Intelligence and Consciousness that knows exactly what you need now. There are untold numbers of higher realms working with each Flame.

Again, this is a concise, simplified teaching of these *Seven Sacred Flames* to allow a faster integration of wisdoms that have been previously brought forward in a more lengthy and detailed fashion. It is an essential aspect of this channel's fragments within his Divine Soul Plan to assist us at this time.

DIVINE DISCUSSIONS

Seven Sacred Flames: Daily Use

From: Adama, Father of Humanity, High Priest of Telos, Lemuria, Inner Earth Civilization.

Dearly Beloved Sisters And Brothers Upon The Surface Of Mother Earth,

Each of us within the Inner Earth Civilizations and you too upon the surface of the planet can use the activity of The Seven Sacred Flames each day of the week. These Flames are one of the most powerful **Ascension Tools** ever gifted to humanity *to assist you in evolving into a higher frequency of existence.* Each day of the week has one essential Flame as a focus:

When we awaken we become aware that we exist and 'will' ourselves into existence; **(Flame#1, Monday).**

Then we can become aware of a 'significant other' in our life: a husband/wife, a lover, an occupation, a planet or pet...this tweaks our consciousness and we begin to see ourselves as reflections of others (or not); **Flame #2, Tuesday.**

We then may begin 'to think' who we are and why we are here (what we were being yesterday and what we are going to be/do today; **Flame #3, Wednesday.**

Then we arise and become aware of our physical body and care for it through: breath, sound, motion, meditation, nutrition and begin to balance our energies; **Flame #4, Thursday.**

We then can become ready to decide what we want to be/do and how to manifest those intentions the best way possible; **Flame #5, Friday.**

Then, if we so choose, we become conscious that by ourselves we can do nothing, that the electrons that maintain and sustain life are the real creator, and we can choose to know that the same electrons are in everything and everyone, 'world servicing' our actions to a higher purpose for the support of others; **Flame #6, Saturday.**

Lastly, we can choose to see and know what affects our actions and affects others and can choose to process ourselves through heightened consciousness. We can recap the day and review the teachings and tools we gained. We can accept ourselves with compassion and forgive all thoughts and actions that caused harm; we now know the fleeting nature of the 3D world. By allowing ourselves to change, we can change the world knowing we are God; **Flame #7, Sunday.**

DIVINE DISCUSSIONS

Sacred Shifts To Ascend

From: Adama, Father of Humanity, High Priest of Telos, Lemuria, Inner Earth Civilization.

Dear Ascending Humanity,

As your planet continues to contract and expand during its final 2,000-year epoch Ascension Process (transmuting from density, returning to Light), humanity is being given wondrous opportunities to also transcend from a dense carbon based reality to Light. This is your Divine Destiny. How and when you achieve your ascension is through your freedom of will and choice. Those who choose not to ascend during planet Earth's final epoch will do so elsewhere.

For those of you who choose your *Sacred Shift* during this final epoch, let us review what is necessary through your relationship with self-mirroring outward to take place. This is a process of inside out. Looking at your outside world is not a measure of the process. You, too, will contract and expand during this Ascension Process, so we ask that you have acceptance, compassion and forgiveness for your process. Remember, dear sisters and brothers, this is a choice you chose (as a soul) in being human. This process is not a form of punishment or trial, but it provides the learning tools necessary to facilitate your mastership to be in world and universal service.

Each Sacred Shift is an energetic intention/vortex/portal/doorway -- representing one of the twelve star systems, which seeded this planet. The final shift is your planet's ascension itself.

Sacred Shifts

1. To achieve this shift, heal all wounds and ego defenses created in past and present lives. You are not your wounds and defenses, but they are ruling your lives and world at this time. There are many tools from higher realms to assist you within your personal process, including many from The Angel News Network and others. This healing will allow your re-connection to higher realms, your Divine Soul Plan (your purpose in being here) and to realize your Divinity.

2. This shift allows you to know the meaning, value and purpose of agreeing to be within this third dimension (3D) of emotions, thoughts and physical reality. Each dimension has a purpose. This 3D is to learn to love through density and duality and to move into world service through unity. To ascend to a higher dimension it is necessary to achieve the higher frequency of that dimension. This means 'being' the higher frequency at all times. The 5D frequencies and beyond are in service to *All There Is*.

3. Through the Ascension Process, your believing mind is moving into service to your knowing heart. Stored within the DNA of your heart is all you have learned from past and present lives. Your self-mastered self is alive and well within your heart, and it is waiting for you to access it.

4. Duality, separation and confrontation are an illusion even though you have chosen to learn from them. It is time to wake up and know there is no two, only one. You can choose to let go of all the pain and suffering this illusion has caused you by knowing you are Love, loved and lovable.

5. All the judgment, shame and blaming in your world is

simply how you feel about yourself reflecting out to others. Once you wake up to your Divinity there can be none of this any longer. Are you ready to receive and give your Divinity?

6. Surrender to not knowing. In the not knowing is everything; all possibilities and probabilities live within the void of Creation. Remember, your knowing heart contains all you need to know. You are learning to access and 'think' with your heart. You are not eliminating your mind, just allowing it to assert what the heart knows.

7. In effect, your ascension is the marriage/union of you and your Higher Eternal Self, called the I AM Presence, the Christ Consciousness. You achieve this union through the healing of the self-centered me into the healed We.

8. The most important aspect of your 'human contract' on planet Earth is to understand, access and apply your Divinity within every moment of the now. The failure to know this is the reason for all the negative matters on your planet. Paradise awaits you to create it.

9. Every human being, animal, plant, mineral and unseen beings on planet Earth are made of the same Cosmic stuff and consciousness as you and have a divine right to be here. They are not meant to be controlled by you. You do not have the right to attempt to control what you did not create nor understand its reasons to be here. Your trying to control everyone and everything on the planet are reflections of your fearful (non-loving) relationship with self.

10. Your emotions are creating the life you are experiencing. Negative emotions stored in the

atmosphere are even creating your weather. Emotions create thoughts, which create actions. Perhaps it is time to eliminate old patterns, habits and rituals that no longer serve your highest good or that of others.

11. The feeling of joy is one of the highest frequencies/vibrations within the universe. Joy is an empowering aspect of Love, the building block of the universe. The feeling of joy allows manifestation with grace and ease. Pay attention to how much joy is presently in your life.

12. Within your Ascension Process, you are moving from density to Light. This process is achieved by two factors: first, know you came from Love, are Love and are lovable and then mirror that out into the world; second, have gratitude for 'what is' in your life rather than focusing on 'what is not.' You are mastering the cosmic equation, gratitude=abundance.

13. Finally, are you willing to do the work to release yourself from yourself? All the tools you need have been given to you from many higher realms many times. Are you ready now to commit to your ascension and see it as the most important aspect of your life and lives?

Assisting Your Ascension, And Our Reunion...

Seven Sacred Steps For Your Ascension

From: Adama, The Father of Humanity, High Priest of Telos, Lemuria, Inner Earth Civilization.

Dear Beloved Humanity Ascending Into Your Divinity,

We, once again, come to you to support your process of ascension having held the wisdom and focus to be and do for eons. We are your pathway Home. As planet Earth continues to activate various portals/vortices within her Ascension Process, this activation affects all within and upon her body.

Let us now review seven steps necessary for humanity to balance and integrate your movement into a higher frequency of existence.

Previously, we have given you concise teachings within the *Seven Sacred Flames* and *Sacred Shifts*. Now these *Seven Sacred Steps* complete the "Sacred Trilogy Of Teachings" essential for the healing of your emotional, mental and physical bodies. This trilogy is a Divine Demonstration of how much you are loved and supported by we higher realms. Know, dear ones, each time one of you moves into your ascension (moving from the me to the We), you create an energetic pathway for others to follow...

Step #1: Express And Release Your Emotions And Thoughts.

Your emotions and thoughts have been ruling your lives and world for far too long. It is time to know you are not your emotions or thoughts. It is vital to know that by experiencing your emotions and thoughts you may release them from your DNA cellular memory. You have been passing along your unexpressed emotions and thoughts lifetime after lifetime. Your emotions and thoughts created the duality and confrontation within your physical bodies and your world at large. It is time to stop learning what is through what is not.

Step #2: Receive The Universal Laws Creating Balance.

Once you master *Step #1*, you are beginning your release from the third dimensional world of emotions and thoughts and will be better able to begin to receive the Universal Laws that balance *All There Is* such as: Giving = Receiving; Masculine = Feminine; Law of Cause and Effect; Law of Karma; Cosmic Love; Law of Attraction; Oneness, etc. All of these Universal Laws have been made available to you in the past and are available to you at present by simply asking for them to be revealed (again).

Step #3: Apply Unconditional Equality, Harmony, Balance And Love For All Life.

Each step energetically builds upon the other in Divine Order. Once *Step #1* and *Step #2* are firmly seated within your consciousness, you are ready to know that all things within and upon this planet have a Divine Right to be here and that you are able to apply unconditional equality, harmony, balance and love for all life. You are learning how to create peace on Earth. Learning and applying acceptance and compassion for all life is vital to your ascension.

Step #4: See Your Wounds And Ego Defenses Without Judgment Or Shame As Learning Tools.

Through Steps 1, 2, and 3, you begin to move into direct relationship with your higher self -- your I AM Presence or Christ Consciousness. You are accepting your multi-dimensionality. Through acceptance and compassion, thus forgiveness, you see your wounds and ego defenses without judgment or shame and have an intense knowing that they are learning tools and are not who you truly are. You are freeing yourself from yourself.

Step #5: Clear All Emotional, Mental And Physical Aspects Of Self.

Here you are ready to clear and cleanse all emotional, mental and physical dense aspects of self that need balancing. You are transmuting your dense carbon self into Light. Each emotion, thought and physical imbalance is readying itself to move into its Light body aspect. You are seeing your Divinity and knowing this is who you truly are. All that has proceeded this moment has merely been a preparation for now.

Step #6: Commit To Being A Master Teacher.

All of the previous steps have been a preparation to know that everything in your lives prepared you to be in (world) service to one another, as a reflection of your self-mastered love of self. You all have the same needs, and that is a mirror of your Oneness- all of you having been created of the same Cosmic Matter. You are becoming ready to commit to being the master teachers of this world and beyond.

Step #7: Join The Realm Of The Ascended Masters.

After you have mastered the first six steps, the higher realms, from whence you came, will purify every energetic component of your being. Your dense man power will have become God Power, Light. You will then be ready to join the realm of the Ascended Masters, your Divine Destiny and destination.

Seven Sacred Flames Chart

From: Adama, The Father of Humanity, High Priest of Telos, Lemuria, Inner Earth Civilization.

Monday: *The Flame Of The Will Of God* (Flame # 1)

Chakra: Throat -- Creative Expression, Expressive Communication, Self-Empowerment, Telepathy

Color: Blue

Archangel Michael; Ascended Master El Morya

Tuesday: *The Flame Of Cosmic Love* (Flame #3)

Chakra: Heart -- Acceptance, Compassion, Empathy, Forgiveness Unconditional Love

Color: Pink

Archangel Chamuel; Ascended Master Paul The Venetian

Wednesday: *Flame Of Healing And Manifestation* (Flame #5)

Chakra: Third Eye (Forehead) -- Higher Realm Sight, Precognitive Dreams, Inspiration, Visualization

Color: Green

Archangel Raphael; Ascended Master Hilarion

Thursday: *Flame Of Resurrection* (Flame #6)

Chakra: Solar Plexus -- Creation Of Self, Perception, Self-Empowerment, Understanding the emotional body in relationship to the mental and physical bodies

Color: Purple & Gold

Archangel Uriel; Ascended Masters Sanada & Lady Nada

Friday: *The Ascension Flame* (Flame #4)

Chakra: Sacral -- Desire (including sexual energy), Intuition, Self-Reliance

Color: White

Archangel Gabriel; Ascended Master Serapis Bey

Saturday: *The Violet Flame Of Transmutation* (Flame # 7)

Chakra: Root (Base Of Spine, Seat Of The Soul) -- Physical Vitality, Sexuality, Survival Instinct

Color: Violet

Archangel Zadkiel; Ascended Master Saint Germaine

Sunday: The Flame Of Illumination & Wisdom (Flame #2)

Chakra: Crown – Enlightenment/Spiritual Perfection, Totality Of BEingness, Undifferentiated Consciousness

Color: Yellow

Archangel Jophiel; Ascended Master Lanto

Seven Aspects Of Ascension

From: Archangel Uriel.

Dear Beloved Humans Ascending Into Ascension,

As you enter into another of your Earth years, it is time to remind you that there are vortices and portals within and upon your planet that are activating in order to assist yourselves and your home planet into a higher frequency of existence called Ascension, your Divine Destiny. This will allow communities of equality, harmony and balance. Your planet is within the final epoch of this process; thus, everything and everyone within and upon the planet is being given the choice through your freedom of will and choice to ascend. Dear ones, no matter how things may appear in your lives or world this process is in progression. Let us now review once again the *Aspects of Ascension* to ensure your journey.

- o You are Divine Eternal Spiritual BEings having a human experience through your free will and choice. Choosing to be human is simply an aspect of your being.

- o There is no right or wrong, good or bad or loss and gain within your Ascension Process. This is simply the way you have chosen to learn what you need to learn the way you chose to do so. Consider not judging or shaming your process.

- o The choice you made to be human is an agreement between you and Creation.

- o Accept with compassion and forgive yourself and

all others you bring into your life as a learning tool. Forgiveness is the pathway beyond separation and duality, which rules your world at present.

- o Remember, your ego housed within your mental body is returning in service to your knowing heart; the mind believes; your heart has stored within its DNA your many lifetimes of learning. It is time to apply them, if you so choose.

- o Remember and come to know the unseen higher realms are supporting you every step of the way. Know and accept your physical death is the last hurdle of your process. You are destined to become Eternal BEings Of Light through the Ascension Process of your home planet.

- o Remember, and hold in your eternal loving heart, you have never been alone and never will be. We are joined together in Divine Oneness, beingness into doingness, and we shall be with you until that Oneness is complete, and then your service to *All There Is* will begin...

Saint Francis Energy

Interview with Saint Francis, Featuring Channel Phillip Elton Collins and Spiritual Journalist Joel Anastasi.

Note: This interview occurred in preparation for a *Divine Discussions* gathering.

Greetings Beloved Brethren,

This is the energy, the Francis energy, the energy that began the soul journey of the channel that we are coming through at present and the pathway of the one you call Pope.

We are an energy of compassion and brotherhood, an energetic balance of the masculine and feminine energies. We are an energy of the inner relationship of all life forms upon this planet—be they human, be they animal, mineral or plant.

We are here to remind humanity all of you are made of the same cosmic material. The same sacred science is involved in the creation of all of you, the same electrons and atoms that create diversified forms of Consciousness, which is the Divine Destiny of each of you -- be you human, animal, plant or mineral.

Joel: Could you tell us more about the energy you represent?

Saint Francis: St Francis is the incarnation of this specific frequency and energy and a messenger of it. There have been various expressions throughout the history of your planet of this particular energy. Most recently what you call the Franciscan orders of priesthood, which is connected with the Melchizedek order or priesthood, which is connected to the White Christ Brotherhood, a light of the Christ Consciousness.

There are many orders that have connected religions and spiritually throughout the evolutionary path of this particular planet.

Joel: Did you say that Pope Francis is an expression of this energy?

Saint Francis: Yes, that is why we are coming through at this time to address your needs within the explanation of his relationship with this energy, dear one.

Joel: I am very impressed by this man. He has caught the attention of the world with many statements and encyclicals and with his behavior generally. His encyclical on global warming is getting a lot of attention from people on all sides of the issue.

Saint Francis: There have been many corrupted influences in that position throughout humanity's history, which you are aware of, as are many other humans. In your vernacular, dear one, he is the 'real deal.' He is a messenger sent of this frequency, a messenger of the people, by the people and for the people. And not only the people but also all other life forms on this particular planet which humanity affects.

One of the reasons his messages of humanity are including weather and the conditions on the planet is because they are all interconnected. He is connecting wisdoms and events of consciousness (or the lack of Consciousness) and how it affects the planet and humanity. He has that wisdom. He has that connection.

Joel: Can you confirm what the Pope is saying about man's role in the warming of the planet?

Saint Francis: There is a combination of interactions between humanity's behavior and the natural evolutionary path of the planet. There are many events taking place on the planet, as a result of what you call an *Ascension Process* of moving from one reality to another, moving from a denser reality to a higher frequency of reality, which is taking place, which is being exacerbated by the behavior, emotions, thoughts and actions of humanity.

In this specific case, this individual you call the Pope is addressing weather and its relationship to humanity's behavior. There is no doubt that humanity's behavior is increasing the evolutionary experience of the planet herself. All of this is reflecting a larger cosmic experience of Oneness and Unity Consciousness that is taking place.

If we pull back from your planet and we pull back farther from your solar system and we pull back further into the galactic experience, you will see that your sister galaxy, your so called Andromeda is moving in close concert with your home galaxy, the Milky Way. They will eventually move into Oneness.

This aspect is also taking place within the planet herself. Your continents are moving closer together. They were together at one time. They separated and are now coming back together within their evolutionary path. Humanity's behavior is affecting that as well.

Joel: So you're saying that the natural cycle the planet is in is increasing temperatures on Earth and man's behavior is exacerbating that?

Saint Francis: Yes, dear one, yes. It is the emotions and thoughts of humanity that are collected within the atmosphere, which affect your weather patterns, your storms, some of your geological activities, such as your volcanic activity and farther out beyond the planet herself.

Joel: Is man's contribution to this trend causing a problem if Earth's temperatures are rising anyway?

Saint Francis: It is not so much the temperature of the planet herself. It is the frequency and the electro-magnetic composition of the frequency brought about by the emotions and thoughts and the density they represent that affects the weather patterns on the planet.

Joel: There is a vast melting underway of ice in both north and south poles, Greenland and elsewhere. To many of us it appears catastrophic.

Saint Francis: It is a great change unknown to you. It doesn't mean that it hasn't happened before. The missing ingredient is the lack of awareness that the planet is a living conscious being and the roles of animals, plants, etc.

Joel: What are the karmic consequences for those who pollute our air, land and water for personal profit, essentially destroying Creation?

Saint Francis: Those who are harming the planet are attempting to control what they did not create. You cannot control what you did not create. Humanity did not create the planet. You were invited here from various realms within the cosmos. As part of your soul plan, you chose to be here.

There is a karmic consequence. It is the way that the cosmos and nature, as you call her, balances and maintains and sustains herself. An example would be the civilization of Atlantis, which was more technologically and spiritually advanced than you are in many ways. They reached a point where they could destroy the planet through their warring, through imposing their masculine assertive energy, the way they thought life should be on this planet and their need to subjugate and attempt to control others, even through the creation of life. As a result of their intention, their civilization was destroyed by dispensations that were received by certain cosmic counsels in order to protect the planet herself.

The planet will not be destroyed as a result of humanity's behavior. There will be a check and balance on that. It is the destiny of this particular planet, which has been a *Divine Experiment*, a 'Lover-versity' if you will, of learning to express Love and all of its forms *of being there and not being there as a Divine Cosmic Experience for the entire universe* to play out.

That has been largely playing itself out for millennia. It has had some respites during some of the Golden Ages, the various seven or eight golden ages on your planet. You are in the process, if you so choose, of finalizing humanity's expression of your final golden age on this planet to return to being Light from whence you came. That is the path. That is the circle of Creation. You come from Light; you return to Light within that process.

Once you return to Light again you can make a decision in concert with other higher realms as to exactly how that energy of Light is to be expressed once again.

Joel: The people who are polluting our Earth and trying to control the political process, can they do that with no karmic consequences to their future soul choices?

Saint Francis: When they leave this frequency, they will experience a balance of what they have created through the intention to harm. These individuals are here for a purpose as well. They are here for a clearing and a cleansing of humanity's wounds and defenses to come up for a review to be fully expressed and experienced. Things may appear more extreme than ever before, but in reality, that is not the case.

You are simply aware of what is taking place in a more forthright way because of the electronic digital communication systems that you have and your transportation systems. So you are more aware of who is doing what than in the past. That doesn't mean the past did not contain more extreme behavior. Humanity has the freedom of will and choice, which the higher realms cannot interfere with unless it means the destruction of the planet herself.

Humanity has the right, if you will, to destroy itself, if it so chooses. It is a preference of the Divine Plan that created humanity that that not take place. Many of you are making individual decisions for that not to take place and that you will ascend to a higher frequency of existence as a result of your individuated soul plans, whether in this lifetime, the next lifetime or the lifetime after that.

Joel: When we experience the mass killings as we did this week in Charleston, South Carolina (SC) and as we have experienced so often in our country, it's easy to think things are not getting better.

Saint Francis: There have been more intense experiences in the past and to a greater degree than what you are describing, dear one. The fact that these are happening at this time and that you are aware of it through the communication systems that have been gifted to you from higher realms, make you more aware of them. Thus, in turn, the collective and the individual can choose to make another decision. Be aware of the healing taking place of the racial divide that something like this demonstrates, which also allows a collective healing and coming together.

Also, dear one, take into consideration as a part of their soul plan the individuals who chose to leave as a part of that particular experience who in your vocabulary you might say, "sacrificed" themselves for the good of the whole. Remember, there are no accidents; there are no coincidences of events. Perhaps each individual was divinely in place where they needed to be at that moment in time in order to gift to humanity, in this particular case, their leaving and what that represents as a healing of the duality and separation of your racial divide within the country you call the United States.

Joel: I suspected that they had made that choice. But it is hard for many of us to understand and accept that kind of self-sacrifice.

Saint Francis: That is the divine organization of Creation, dear one, and humanity is still in the process of becoming aware of this -- trusting it and committing to that process.

Joel: As you were saying it gives us a chance to make another choice, I thought of the call by many in SC to remove the Confederate flag from the State Capitol

Building. Many people have seen that flag as a symbol of white supremacy.

Saint Francis: The portal of your so-called SC was a gateway for slavery into your country. It is a vortex of slavery. It was a point of entry within the historical events of your United States. The reason this is happening in this particular geographic location is to heal the karmic consequences seeded within this particular portal, this particular vortex of this state called South Carolina. It is an opportunity to release the karmic consequence, the cause and effect, that is in the DNA of that specific location.

Joel: Consistent with that healing, I have been so moved by the statements of forgiveness that were coming from that church congregation and from people who had friends and family members killed.

Saint Francis: So what gift does that forgiveness, that acceptance with compassion send to the rest of humanity?

Joel: Love and forgiveness.

Saint Francis: Yes, it allows them to make another choice. So that is a good example of what is taking place there. It isn't a coincidence that forgiveness is coming from those individuals who experienced what you would call this tragedy. It is an opportunity for the rest of humanity to see exactly where they are within their spiritual foundation of truth and connection to Creation and connection to their God, realizing that the ones they freed through themselves, through this forgiveness, is themselves.

This does not mean that there will not be a karmic consequence for the individual who brought this event upon humanity, but also take into mind the soul plan of the individual who made the decision to be this individual to bring this harm upon these others. And you can stretch that out further and further into your histories, and you can see other examples of individuals who played those roles within the evolution of humanity and begin to see the Divine Design, if you will, the organization of how creation actually works through the interactions of individuals, be they negative or positive.

Joel: Many people believe the Vatican has had a long history of separation and has been a part of the controlling of the many by the few. Can you say something about Pope Francis's mission in relation to the idea of changing the behavior of the Vatican as a religious organization?

Saint Francis: As we said at the beginning of this message, he is an instrument and a messenger of the St. Francis energy, if you will, of peace, love, acceptance to humanity and of all of the life forms on this planet. That is his focus. He has chosen and been chosen to be a frequency of this particular energy. That is why we are coming in at this time. He has chosen to go into the belly of the beast, if you will. And, yet, at the same time keep himself in it and not of it knowing that his role is to begin to affect and transcend and to transition the intention and the focus of this endeavor you call church. He realizes that all that may not take place within his incarnational cycle.

But he knows he is planting a seed of change, and without that change, without the truth, goodness, love and support that he brings in to it, he also realizes that the endeavor itself cannot succeed or continue as it is. It will fall upon itself in the corruption of itself. So, in effect, he is bringing in a new light. He is bringing in an old foundation of truth and love into the newness of it. He is asking that it return to being a church of the people, which in reality it never has been.

It has been an instrument of control. It has been an instrument of the disempowerment of the feminine energy. It has hidden many of the historical and spiritual truths of the reality of humanity and your true history on this planet. He is laying a pathway for all of that to be opened. For within the vaults and libraries of this endeavor is much of the truth of which we speak, and he knows (how) to bring it out, step by step, knowing that it is a pathway of acceptance.

He is aware of the resistance within and outside the organization that will resist the changes he is asking for. But he knows within his soul plan that he has chosen and been chosen, if you will, to bring this truth into this powerful organization that will mean the continued life and breath of it with these changes in place. Without it, it will fall upon itself.

Joel: What might we do to help his efforts?

Saint Francis: Much of humanity is 'getting it' about this individual, dear one. It is interesting to note that much of that awareness is coming from outside of the endeavor of which he is a part. So he has struck a collective chord, if you will, in addition to the internals of the organization. Ironically, his support is coming from outside rather than inside his organization. And it is the pressures, shifts, and changes to the intentions of goodness coming from outside in that can affect a dynamic of inside out.

Joel: It's interesting that the Pope is scheduled to address the U.S. Congress in September, which is controlled by our Republican Party which reacted quite negatively to the encyclical, essentially saying, keep your comments to religious matters.

Saint Francis: There are many within your so-called Congress who do not understand the educational and scientific training that this divine soul has had. He has come to this position as Pope fully prepared for what he needs to speak to humanity and for those who will be in opposition to him. He is a scientist within his own right, not simply a head of a church.

Joel: Not only is he a chemist and a scientist, but he turned to an impressive team of scientific authorities in preparing this encyclical. This is not simply the product of his own efforts.

Saint Francis: Again, he has the support of many outside the endeavor you call "church." The church as it is structured within humanity at this time is an endeavor outside of the individual's soul plan. True church exists within the heart of the individual and radiates outside that heart energy from inside out.

The distortion of this church has been the attempt to control what it had not created. Thus, there truly can be no control. You can subjugate. You can keep the forces down for a certain period of time, but then there will be revolution, if you will, in order for humanity to accept the reality that each of you is a Divine Spiritual Being having this human experience. The expression is an inside out process.

It doesn't mean that organizations cannot support that, but they cannot replace it and be effective long term. That day of reckoning is upon humanity.

Joel: Would it be accurate to call you the Francis energy?

Saint Francis: You may call us whatever you resonate with: The Francis energy. There will be those who will not resonate with the term St. Francis. But, understand, these are simply names that your languages have given these frequencies of consciousness that do not exist for us. They are simply a nomenclature for you to be able to identify us whether it is Archangels Michael, Gabriel, Uriel, Raphael, Mother Mary or whatever. But, if you so choose, you may call us the Francis energy.

Joel: I'm familiar with the Archangelic Realms and the Mary energy. What is the Francis energy in relation to those? Do you have a separate mission as they do?

Saint Francis: We are very connected to the ascension and evolutionary path of the planet and all life forms upon it. We work in concert with Archangel Uriel who is your world teacher. We work with the elementals. We work with the soul plans of humanity. Many of you are aware of our relationship with the animals. That extends to the minerals and the plants as well, and all who have chosen to be here as guardians of the planet, which allows humanity to maintain and sustain life here.

Joel: Would you like to give us a closing statement?

Saint Francis: Be aware of what a magnificent time it is upon your planet. Be aware that as things may appear to be becoming worse that there is a clearing and a cleansing taking place. Be aware that your planet is involved in a cosmic evolutionary path of ascension moving into a Light body, a star, a sun, if you will; thus, in turn, everything within and upon her body is within that process as well. You have chosen, as being human, to be a part of that process. You are all here for that experience.

Be aware of the power of your emotions and your thoughts. Be aware of your empowerment of self, that *you are individuated soul plans* having this human experience. Be aware of the events that are taking place in life. They are not always as they appear through their mental interpretation to what they are. Be aware that there is a Divine Plan in place that the universe in concert with energies such as ours knows exactly how to balance, maintain, and sustain balance with Cosmic and Earth reality.

Be aware that your freedom of choice is a Divine Gift, and you can always make another choice from the ones you are making now. Be aware that you may simply ask to connect with us, and by simply asking you shall receive, dear ones. And so it is.

Separating From Separation Into Oneness

From: Council of Archangelic Realms (CAR).

Dear Beloved Human Beings, Being So Human,

Many of you know we of the Angelic Realms, throughout your chaotic history, have loved and supported humanity through the many often challenging learning-tools aspects of choosing to be human. Now with the ascension of your planet and your species moving into another higher frequency of existence, it is crucial that you make another choice to end separation, if you so choose.

We cannot interfere with your freedom of choice and will, but we can once again bring wisdoms to assist you in making a choice different from the ones of the past and present.

The basic variable at this time continues to be your lack of applied knowledge leading into wisdom, understanding and knowing **We Are All One**. We are all built of the same energy of Cosmic Love, and we express that love in many diversified ways. *Seeing the Oneness throughout the diversity is the challenge for most.* Because we may look and sound different, it does not mean we are different. **This is the mystery of Creation to resolve: understanding the relationship of You, Oneness, and** *All There Is*, **reflected within your relationship with Self (a reflection of ALL).**

This is a very challenging reality for much of humanity to accept due to your erroneous belief systems created by those who have attempted to control and separate you in the past and present.

Let us see if we can present the above abstractions in a more simplified way: Everything comes from the same *'Cosmic stuff'* but chooses a diversified, individual uniqueness. We all initially come from energy and through the consciousness of that energy, we choose how to express it. How we choose to express this energy is called *life*. There are limitless expressions of life even on your own planet, which you are still discovering.

Since you chose to be human (and you did, since you are Creation creating), this is how you chose to learn about 'self', the reflection of *All There Is*. This is why the wisdom, *"the only relationship you are having is the one with self,"* is so vital to understand and apply. This is why **healing self and mirroring that inside out** is so vital at this time. What you have now is wounded, unhealed 'selves', individuals running your world. **Your world's dense energy will simply not be allowed into higher realms as you transcend/ascend into higher frequencies of existence.**

There is no shaming, blaming or judgment within higher frequencies, which are such a preferred aspect of your reality at present. The only expectation for your advancement is to be and know the conscious creation of **Oneness** through your emotions, thoughts and physical form as human. Through the activation of your soul plan (purpose in being here) and your expressed unique talents and gifts you can be in service to all those around and in your world.

As shared in the past, humanity divides into thirds. One-third is awake and intends to ascend and assist others; another third is in resistance and intends to hold onto the old, and the final third is not awake and has no idea what is going on. We of the higher realms are here to assist all of you in your awakening since you have been asleep a long time, and time is running out. Remember, your planet is within the final 2,000-year cycle of transmuting from carbon-based reality back to Light (and so are you).

As you learn more about yourself, your experiences and definitions of reality change through your awakening to ever expanding new truths, which replace erroneous beliefs of the past and present. As you transcend the fear, doubt and ignorance of the past, it becomes impossible for the few to control the many through deceit and denial of the deceit.

For those who choose not to awaken and stay in resistance, they will be given all the time they need to transcend/ascend. They just won't do it on this planet. They will be given the opportunity within other galaxies and upon other planets. They will ascend. It is just a matter of how and when. The Divine Destiny of this planet is to ascend to a higher frequency of existence with all life upon and within its body doing the same.

For now, our focus is with you who resonate with what is being said through your discernment (think with your heart) and are ready to apply and commit to the wisdom being shared. Remember to apply your resonance (resonate with your heart) and discernment with all matters of information received. Do not apply it if you do not resonate with this message.

Through resonance and discernment you can begin to build communities of equality, harmony and balance based upon mastering and loving self. We of the higher realms will never stop loving and supporting you until you have achieved your Divine Destiny/destination of Oneness in service to All There Is.

More and more you will attract individuals whose lives resonate and discern with 'We' consciousness rather than 'Me' consciousness because it brings them joy. Your emoted feelings are your 'ticket' to your Divinity. Through your various unique talents and gifts, you will begin to effect a frequency shift around you. Like-mindedness, like spiritedness, allows your community to grow and expand, bringing more and more truth into your lives, thus, creating the life you want rather than the one that exists.

When this happens, it creates love-force energy that also feeds we of the higher realms, balancing giving and receiving. This allows us to send more love and support to you.

Everything that you are creating in your lives are the learning tools you need to learn what you need to learn the way you need to learn it to now create a permanent healing. It is time to take responsibility for all this, thereby, eliminating victimhood by accepting with compassion and forgiving how you have chosen to learn. By knowing who you are and why you are here, you create a self-empowering foundation upon which to build a new life and world. The energy that makes this possible is self-love mirrored out to others.

Remember, the reason you chose to be here was to learn to love (the building block of all) while being human on planet Earth, the 'Lover-versity' from which you have not yet graduated. It is Love, Cosmic Consciousness, which brought you all here. When you are within the frequency of Love (the highest frequency in Creation) you vibrate at that frequency, which means you entrain to the highest frequency within any environment). Love frequency has no limit and can grow and expand endlessly. Whether another is able to receive and give love depends upon what frequency they are vibrating within. You are in the process of remembering and mastering frequency technology. **You are in the process of mastering being Love no matter whether others can receive it or not.**

In this channel's publication, *God's Glossary: A Divine Dictionary*, the **core of love** is defined as "the expression and revelation of your being; showing and sharing all of who you are with life, with the world and every other human being; **love is God being you.**"

Some of the feelings and actions you call love are not Love. Some of them are 'giving to get' while others are about control. The way you express Love depends upon your personal process of knowing who you are and why you are here. If you cannot imagine life without another person or thing, that really is not love. Those emoted strong feelings are based upon fear (an absence of Love) of losing what you think you need. This fear-factored-love reveals a lack of self-love. This is a process of love outside in, rather than inside out. When you have truly learned to love self, you can access the Oneness and the sheer joy of life, being able to be alone without being lonely. Many of you are in the process of mastering this self-love leading to Divine Love, which vibrates freely and is available to everyone all the time.

Through your freedom of choice and will, each day you get to decide to love or not, no matter what is transpiring in your life or world. Remember, through

Love the positive transmutes the negative. You are not here to survive life but to enjoy it. Become conscious of your emotions and thoughts that create your reality all the time. **Keeping your frequency high requires you constantly paying attention to your intention and how you respond rather than react to life.** Then you know how to raise your frequency when it has lowered by **being aware of your emotions and thoughts.**

A good way to maintain and sustain your frequency is to focus on '**what is**' rather than '**what is not**'. Remember, gratitude equals abundance as Cosmic Law. You are the one through your freedom of will and choice deciding at all times how your life will be.

Feeling your feelings is all part of being human. You are not your feelings, but you need to **express them to release them**; otherwise, they create imbalances within your body, creating dis-ease. Not expressing your feelings is actually a form of untruthfulness.

If it resonates, let us choose to express the true emotion of Love (especially to your children, many of whom have the gifts to *way show* your way). The higher realms advanced civilizations be and do this all the time and have created worlds of which you dream to aspire. Let us make and take the time and effort to give Love and support to one another at all times. This is the reason WE exist. As we began this message, since we are all one and what affects one affects all, let us remember it is much easier and more effective to love! And you are going to love the outcome.

Some Ways To Love More

From: Archangel Uriel, World Teacher And Guardian.

- **Allow** others to be heard; listen without thinking what you are going to say next.
- **Speak** without judgment, shaming or blaming (a reflection of self).
- **Give** without the need to get.
- **Consider** connecting to higher realms more often.
- **Respond** without reacting.
- **Balance** giving and receiving.
- **Focus** on 'what is' with joy.
- **Trust** and surrender to not knowing.
- **Accept** with compassion, thus forgive.
- **Remember** your and other's Divinity.

Spirituality And/Or Religion

From: Archangel Uriel, World Teacher And Guardian.

Dear Beloved Humans Being Human,

As you are evolving within your Ascension Process of moving into your Divine Destiny of a higher frequency of existence (creating communities of equality, harmony and balance), you are currently within a personal and cultural transition from human made religions and your true universal spirituality.

Your religions have largely been created on the premise that you needed to reach outside self in order to connect with God, Source or *All There Is*. While your religions have often been based upon some spiritual truth and have done some positive and negative things in your world, their foundation has also been based upon corrupted truth and an attempt to control what they did not create: you and your world.

Your destiny is to free yourselves from forces that attempt to deny who you truly are and why you are here. *You are Divine Eternal Spiritual BEings* having chosen to have a human experience, expressing your talents and gifts through world service, creating unity consciousness. No matter how things may appear in your outside world, your freedom is in process.

Religions have largely been based upon fear, noting: If you do not do 'this' or be 'this' you will suffer (go to hell). *Spirituality is based upon unconditional, Cosmic Love* knowing there is no judgment, shaming or blaming of self. All that you create (and you are the creator of your life) are learning tools to allow further embracement of your spirituality: *you are Creation experiencing itself*. This truth has been hidden from you for eons. If you so choose, it is time to make another choice.

At present, you are seeing attempted change within some of your world religions. Through the cyber-communication systems we have gifted to you, you are seeing these religions experiencing great internal upheaval. This is all a Divine Process to set you free from any endeavor that is not based upon universal spiritual truth. Religions are being given the opportunity to transmute into truth.

This is a time for needed clearing and cleansing of the forces that have held humanity in slumber. Your grand awakening is upon you, dearly beloved humans. This is a loving process of inside out, not outside in.

Summer Solstice Letter

From: Mother Earth.

Dear Beloved Children Upon The Surface Of My Body,

This longest day of the year is another gift to you from your Mother Earth to give you more time to think about your abuse of one another and the planet that is your home, to see the factors that affect both. For those of you who are not aware of it, I AM a conscious living BEing (like yourselves) and my organs (air, water, minerals, oil/gas) are the elements that maintain and sustain my life and your ability to live upon my body. It is essential to your survival that there be a balance that reflects your relationship with yourself and others that allows knowing how and when to use my organs. This can be achieved through creating communities of equality, harmony and balance knowing there is enough for all. When the forces (twelve star systems) came together to create this planet, they intended there would always be enough for all.

As a result of humanity's disconnect (the human mind thought it could do it a better way), from the additional higher realms (Archangelic, Inner Earth Civilizations, Ascended Masters, Star Realms) that also support your survival, you have continued for eons allowing the few to control the many.

This planet has activated a *Divine Soul Plan Ascension Process* (moving from carbon back to Light); thus, all upon the planet will transmute into that same frequency. In effect, the planet is becoming a Light-bodied star, and so are you! The planet will survive

DIVINE DISCUSSIONS

(complete its Divine Soul Plan) no matter what choice humanity makes. So what do you choose?

Through your freedom of choice and will, we ask that you ponder during this longest day of the year the present and future choices you would like to make about yourself, others, those you choose to govern this planet and the endeavors attempting to control something they did not create.

If you so choose, it is time to stop giving your power away to those who do not support the highest good of you and your planet. What do you choose, and how do you plan to implement your choice? The tools to use are your internal gyro system, your resonance (how you feel about something) and your discernment (how you think about something). Remember, *you are much more powerful than you think!*

Alphabetical Listing Of Articles: T

Ten Tenets Of BEingness:
Cosmic Commandments
The Cause And Cure For Terrorism
The Divine Gift Of Dreams
The Gift Of Commitment
The Meaning Of Life
The Returning Of Oneness
The Year Of The Starseed, 2016
Twelve Codes Of Consciousness

DIVINE DISCUSSIONS

Ten Tenets Of BEingness: Cosmic Commandments

From: Council Of Archangelic Realms (CAR).

Dear Beloved Humans,

Michaelmas (September 29th) is the celebration of the Archangels Michael, Gabriel, Raphael and Uriel guarding and guiding humanity. This day especially recognizes Lord Michael who is assisting your advancement from your believing mind to your knowing heart. As your planet releases another 'out breath' at your time of equinox, a time to review your harvest of the past year, we now gift you with the *Ten Tenets Of BEingness: Cosmic Commandments* to set you free from yourselves.

1. Know that *this living, conscious planet and all upon and within her are sacred*; not taking responsibility for this truth will result in her and your physical *but not* spiritual death.

2. Maintain and *sustain connection to the higher realms* from whence you came; not doing so will ultimately lead to your physical demise and spiritual truth.

3. Know *you are each other in disguise*; see the mirror of self in all; not being/doing so will continue your separation and confrontation until you have had enough of it.

4. Be and do together in honoring *the diversity of your Oneness,* allowing the good of all to manifest.

5. *Balance giving and receiving* through compassion

wherever need exists; there is plenty for everyone.

6. *Your heart knows the authentic thing* to be and do in every moment, no matter what the mind is saying.

7. *Honor your body* temple that houses (for now) your Eternal Soul returning to spirit through your emotions and mind creating your reality.

8. *Be truthful and transparent* all the time by knowing your truth, needs and boundaries, through knowing who you are and why you are here; your soul plan and purpose in being here.

9. By *taking full responsibility* for your actions, the reality you create, you eliminate consequences of learning not to your liking.

10. *Know you are Creation experiencing itself* in order to be in world and universal service.

DIVINE DISCUSSIONS

The Cause And Cure For Terrorism

From: Adama, The Father Of Humanity.

Dear Beloved Children Upon The Surface Of Planet Earth,

We of the Inner Earth Civilizations come to you at this crucial time within your evolutionary personal process of moving into a higher frequency of existence (ascension, your divine birthright). This is an inside-out process of healing the relationship with self, self being all there is.

Having once dwelled upon the surface of this planet on the vast advanced **Lemurian continent** and having experienced all that you are now, we intend to support you from our higher realm perspective and existence.

Once again you find yourselves experiencing upheaval and chaos within your world because of your unhealed relationship with self, thus with others. Your world is currently learning *what is* through *what is not* through increased duality, separation and confrontation. It is time, if you so choose, to master the cause and effect and cure of what you call "terrorism." Needing to learn the way you have been learning is coming to an end – no matter how things appear on the outside. What you see and are experiencing is a major clearing and cleansing of the unhealed self.

Once you **understand the cause of so-called terrorism** and realize it is being fueled by hidden forces who intend to keep you in separation and confrontation, you can decide, if you so choose through your freedom of will and choice, to make another choice in healing what you call "terrorism."

As many of you have been taught, love is the force of all Creation. **The purpose of this planet is to learn to love (Christ Consciousness) self first, and foremost, and to allow that love to mirror to others** in order to create communities of equality, harmony and balance, allowing world service through We Consciousness/Oneness.

What you are experiencing in your world today is a lack of love creating lack and limitation throughout your world. This allows the few to attempt to control the many (realizing ultimately you cannot control what you did not create).

Taught wounded feelings of not being good or worthy enough cause many people to have unmet basic needs because they have not been assimilated into their various societies. Through this negative relationship with self, these people become isolated and do not become part of their society or see themselves as part of the Whole (part of the Oneness of everything). This isolation builds upon itself and under certain circumstances can develop into extreme unhealed behavior (especially if others are fueling it) such as terrorism **motivated by hopelessness**. "Nobody loves me and never will so I have nothing to lose but to act out." This is the ultimate form of self-sabotage projected onto others.

The consciousness of these people needs to shift before they can truly know what they need. They are not able to receive until they wake up. Thus, they stay within a blind spot of acting out. These individuals will stay within this vortex of drama until they are ready to commit to changing.

In the meantime, your chosen leaders can begin to focus

on the hidden forces that are fueling the negative actions, which are creating separation and control through confrontation. As you say, "follow the money." You might be surprised where the funding for these many destructive actions originates. So let us discuss giving assistance to those who are able to balance giving and receiving.

We of the higher realms have gifted humanity with many tools and teachings throughout the eons to improve your relationship with self so that you may reflect that onto others. The channel we are coming through at this time is part of an endeavor called The Angel News Network, which is filled with wisdoms from a higher perspective to assist you in healing the relationship with self that then allows constructive interpersonal relationships with others.

Once you begin to love and support others, this behavior teaches others to be and to do the same, and you begin to create a worldwide community of consciousness, building communities of equality, harmony and balance. You then begin to understand the importance of balancing giving and receiving as a cosmic law, as well as balancing the masculine and feminine energies.

The imbalances between giving and receiving and between male and female energies are the root cause of your duality, separation and confrontation. Many cosmic equations, tenets, codes and universal laws are now available to you to heal what needs to be healed. Remember, all of this is the way humanity has chosen to learn what it needs to learn (to love) the way it needs to learn it. By using the above tools, you can more fully activate your *individual soul plans* (your reason to be here).

Through your unique talents and gifts, you can begin to support others, teaching them how to also support others, thus **creating a circular vortex of energy**. This can lead to creating a new paradigm shift for the entire world of Unity/Oneness Consciousness. This process is taking place no matter how you think things appear in your outside world. How and when you achieve it is up to you. You all came from the same Cosmic stuff and are in the process of returning to it (Love and Light).

As more of you wake up through the circular **love vortex of energy**, more joy and happiness is created, allowing hopelessness to become replaced by **self-empowerment through love.** You are beginning to see the meaning, value and purpose of your expressed feelings as empowering tools. Those who felt hopeless are transformed, allowing them to create communities of equality, harmony and balance through their unique talents and gifts. If you are not aware of your talents and gifts, there are many tools to assist you. (See *Life Mastery, A Guide For Creating The Life You Want And The Courage To Live It* by Joel D. Anastasi.)

Others who were not given a chance to participate in their societies in the past now can have an opportunity to contribute, which will benefit themselves and others. All of this begins with one person at a time. Each of you matters. The world would be incomplete without each of you, or you would not be here. When was the last time someone told you that?

Another powerful tool to assist you in creating the world you say you want is your I AM Presence. This is your God presence within you, your Divine Self, and the origin of your soul just above physical form, you as the creator. Say:

"I AM a Divine Spiritual Being choosing to have a human experience right now. I AM aware that all life forms on this planet are conscious beings and have a right to be here. I AM aware I cannot control what I did not create."

When you place the words "I AM" in front of a sentence, it immediately connects you to your higher self and higher realms.

Many things, which you are preparing yourselves to know and to be in the future (about creation and life), are not currently understood. In the meantime, surrender to not knowing. That will allow the possibilities and probabilities to come forth. Quiet your mental bodies that always want to know. You have created the world that exists through your erroneous belief systems and lack of knowing.

Prior to coming here, you all agreed to a 'human contract.' This contract contained your Divine Soul Plan (your reason to be here) and fully defined your talents and gifts. Some of you know your soul plan and are aware of your talents and gifts. Some of you are still discovering the truth about you. Either way is perfect. There is no right or wrong, better or worse way to fully experience you (Creation expressing itself). **When this human contract is fully expressed, there can be no terrorism.**

When you are not conscious of your soul plan or your purpose in being here, you see yourself as not good or worthy enough to make a difference in the world. The wounded and defended self will ask, "What can one person possibly do?" If you choose through your freedom of will, it is time to know and act on the wisdom (applied knowledge) that **your being here does matter.**

It is time to apply your talents and gifts contained in your soul plan to **create the life and world you say you want** -- in effect, create a new world paradigm of Oneness where each of you matters.

Begin to shift the mental body *belief* that you do matter into the *knowing* heart that knows you are the Creator creating and that **you do matter in matter.** As more people become aware of this truth, you will create a quantum shift and begin creating communities of equality, harmony and balance. You will **begin to see everyone and everything as an aspect of yourself** -- other humans, animals, plants and minerals. You will begin to see the planet herself as a conscious living BEing whose organs are the air, water, oil, gas and minerals.

You will begin to know the essential importance of wisdom and to begin to honor all life, especially the gift of the elders. Within advanced civilizations where we have lived for thousands of years, the elder wisdom is the keystone of our lives. In your world you often take the declining body of the elder and 'warehouse' them within old folk's facilities, rather than value what they can teach (especially to the young). You are taking one of the most vital parts of your lives (your elders) and, in effect, throwing them away. This is a form of insanity. If you so choose, begin to see your elders as beacons of Light to guide you along your pathway through their past experiences.

The cycles of life, birth, childhood, adulthood and elder are like your planet's seasons. Each has a purpose for being and doing. No matter which cycle you find yourself in, that cycle can bring grace and joy into your life and the lives of others. This is why these cycles were created. You are in the process of preparing yourselves to become immortal beings. Honoring your life cycles is a true path to that eternal existence.

Please know that your concept of terrorism is based upon a lack of understanding of your integrated **We Consciousness of Oneness**. You are, in effect, moving from the me to the We by healing the relationship with self, reflecting *All There Is*.

Remember, this life and all the lives you have had on this beautiful planet have all been learning tools to teach and support all of which we share at this time. Wake up, dear humanity, and know **you are Divine Spiritual Beings having a human experience to master being human and to transcend into the Eternal BEing of Love and Light that you are!**

The Divine Gift Of Dreams

From: Akashic Records.

Humanity presently lives and exists within the third dimension of emotions, thoughts and physical bodies. When asleep, humans move into a disembodied fourth dimension (with no time nor distance) of the astral or psychic where dreams reside. Let us now have a discussion of the meaning, value and purpose of these mystical aspects of humanity. Can it be true that each human has a gift from the gods, a built in gyro guidance system, through dreams? Throughout history, as a species on earth, humanity has queried the meaning of dreams endlessly. **Perhaps it is time now to know the truth about what dreams are and why they exist within humanity's BEingness as human beings.**

The truth is if you know how to access and use your dreams, they can give you insightful, supportive information about almost every aspect of your conscious and unconscious lives, as well as an understanding of the true reality of the universe. *It is curious that an aspect of yourselves (your dreams) that many often do not remember, or believe, can exist to serve your highest good.*

Is it possible as humanity further raises its frequency, thus consciousness, it is waking up to an often hidden powerful aspect that happens when asleep? Today the study of dreams (their interpretation) is growing and expanding as you accept your unseen portions, becoming valuable components of the seen. Perhaps you are beginning to realize that the part you know the least about, the unseen parts, are the most essential aspects of all! Are you ready to review and apply the insights of your dreams?

Learning how to apply your dream insights can actually have a powerful effect on future dreams. The Akashic Records reveals that this power is limitless. This teaching/message is given to humanity to choose, or not, to value dreams as a tool to assist humanity within their evolutionary process of moving into We Consciousness.

Let us examine the fourth dimensional **energetic structure of dreams** to better understand how they really work. The basis of dreams is within emotions and thoughts, which create the third dimensional reality all the time.

Visualize your emotional and mental bodies as a cosmic wheel with spokes coming off from the hub/center of the wheel. At the end points of each spoke are humanity's individuated consciousness, emotions and thoughts. On the opposite side of this end point are humanity's unconscious emotions and thoughts, closed to awareness. All the wheel spokes are connected at the wheel hub/center with each other, allowing conscious and unconscious selves to communicate/connect. The wheel hub/center itself is the multi-conscious emotion/mind of *All There Is/Creation* which connects to the Akashic Records, the Universal wisdom of all *Creation*, known and unknown. As this cosmic wheel is energetically activated (moves/rotates) through the shift from third to fourth dimensions this is how you access your dreams (through this Divine Design). You are completely unaware of this process, which further reveals the perfection of the creation of humanity and the universe. In truth, humanity is mostly unaware of what is happening within and around them most of the time. But whether humanity is aware or not, life experiences enter this cosmic wheel to be reviewed/revealed within dreams and later in conscious lives, if humans so choose through their freedom of choice and will. **This is the Divine Gift of dreams.** This cosmic wheel becomes a storehouse, mirroring the Akashic Records, which stores everything.

Deep meditation, hypnosis and practice (write down your dreams and study later) can bring the unaware into the aware. So it is the unconscious emotions and mind that awaken when humanity sleeps (in effect, when you are asleep you are awake, and when you are awake you are asleep). So as you awaken when asleep true insights and guidance and other needed healing, individual and global information and forewarnings can be received. Since there is neither time nor distance in the dream realm, the past and future are presented in the now.

Through practice you can learn to decipher when and how to use the information within the dream. It is essential to learn what is happening in the dream and what is happening within your conscious life and connect the two (this is what the mechanics of the cosmic wheel explained earlier does). This is an intuitive process by actually seeing the patterns in the dreams that connect with daily awakened life. *Looking for the truths in the unseen world of dreams can be revealed within awakened and unawakened states of being through practice and accepting with compassion the gift of dreams.*

As in all matters in life, using your discernment (how you think about it) and your resonance (how you feel about it) are also important within the interpretation of dreams. You can always compare what you receive within your dream from other sources as well. **Dreams are not here to hurt or frighten you but to be a storehouse of loving guidance and information to assist in the process of being human.** When humanity further learns how to tap into the reservoir of dreams, life can become a richer, more joyful, mystical experience. As humanity further awakens as a species, the Divine Gift of dreams spreads globally, and humanity learns more and more the meaning, value and purpose of simply remembering dreams.

The Gift Of Commitment

From: Phillip Elton Collins.

Until you are fully committed, there is fear, doubt and ignorance and the chance to:

Mask behind your wounds and ego defenses.

Be and do who you truly are not.

Not be who you truly are and not act upon why you are here (your soul plan).

Kill countless manifestations of Creation and prevent understanding *one elementary truth:* **You are the Creator creating.**

When you consciously commit yourself:

Higher realms connect with your Higher Self.

The unknown becomes the source of all possibilities and probabilities.

Through your WHO and WHY you allow what, how, when and where.

A pathway clears through grace and ease that no human ever dreamed before.

Decisions are made through your intention and Divine intervention.

You know your feelings, thoughts and actions are the countenance of Creation, your Commitment.

The Meaning Of Life

From: Cosmic Keepers Of Creation.

Dear Beloved Humans,

All life has meaning. We, The Cosmic Keepers Of Creation, sense a need to discuss the meaning of life at this time. This need reflects a disconnect from whence life comes and that humanity has not yet understood or agreed on how or why you are creating life.

Many of you have had thousands of lifetimes on this planet, and you have been so completely wrapped up in them that you have not understood the true and deeper meaning/understanding of life. *The lack of trust in the true meaning of life reflects the energy of the original and present collapse/consciousness of humanity.* Your experiences ever since this lack of trust developed has created your lack and limitation, duality, separation and confrontation of your past and present existence. Your mental ego body's need to always be in control or right or wrong (where in reality there is neither) has created much of your pain moving into long term suffering.

Now, if you so choose, it is time, through acceptance, compassion and forgiveness of how you have chosen to learn what you need to learn, to regain your trust and the reunion of you and Creation, creating life. If you so choose, it is the time to regain your trust in who you really are and why you are here.

After many lifetimes, there is no longer trust in the union of you and the creation of life. The monsters of mankind are fear, doubt and ignorance. Now, through the Ascension Process of humanity and your planet (moving to a higher frequency of existence), you are being given the opportunity to regain and relearn the energy of trust in spite of how your world appears at present. It is time to free yourselves from yourselves, if you so choose, through your freedom of choice and will.

What you see in your world at present is you are learning your lessons in ways that are more dramatic -- through inequality, lack of harmony, terrorism, imbalance of masculine and feminine energies, imbalance of giving and receiving, etc. (leaning what is through what is not). Events will continue to be dramatic until humanity learns to make other choices through your free will. This also includes how you abuse the planet herself. The final Golden Age of returning to Light/Oneness, being created during this final 2000 cycle of planet Earth, does not include what your governmental and religious leaders are projecting but will be a life in complete Divine Union with the God-Power within you and with the Creator. It is your destiny that *Divine Order* will be restored; how and when you achieve it is up to you!

Remember, dear humans, what appears as upheaval, painful and often not fair events are mirrors of the consciousness/awareness of the individual and collective people. Your emotions and thoughts are creating your reality through your actions all the time. What you call *acts of god are simply the planet's way of cleansing your abuse*.

Everything that happens, be it personal or global, mirrors the imbalanced or repressed energy of the individual or collective people. The problem is that humanity has not yet understood or accepted how you are creating life. You are creating constantly with your emotions and thoughts, words, and actions (and your silent, unspoken internal dialogue with self). In effect, all human interactions have meaning, value and purpose for self and others, or they would not be there.

Please know and remember, dear humans, that your reason (your Divine Soul Plan) to be on this planet is to activate your soul plan (your purpose/mission in being here). Each and every one of you is needed to be here, or you would not be here (even though your wounds and ego defenses may often tell you, "You are not good enough or worthy enough to be here)." You and life have meaning (learning to love) and your interactions with self and others make an essential difference in the world. Your state of BEingness (rather than doingness), your compassion and empathy for self and others have the ability to create communities of equality, harmony and balance. In effect, each one of you has an archetype soul plan of human experiences (talents and gifts) that can demonstrate the empowerment and need of each and every soul.

*So let's look a little closer at this truth that **each and every one of you is needed and has purpose in being here** (even though at times you feel this is not so). Let's pull back from the micro of life into the macro of existence. Why do you think that your world and you were created? **You and your world were created so that Creation could experience itself more fully by you becoming the Creator yourself. The purpose of your creation is that you would through an Ascension Process increase your vibration and level of consciousness where you can bring the consciousness of energy/spirit into matter to become the Creator. Thus, THE MEANING OF***

LIFE is an interactive evolutionary personal process allowing humans to be able to actively participate in the ever-expanding process of Creation. This allows man power to become God Power through your participation with self and others (learning to fully love self, thus others). This process will create communities of equality, harmony and balance leading to world service. Since each of you is unique, you each have a personalized role in life by learning who you are and why you are here. There are many higher realms teachings (The Angel News Network and others) to assist you in further discovering the who and why of you.

Your soul plan (purpose in being here) is a divine, dynamic connection between your unique talents and gifts and the needs of self, others and the world. Again, there are many higher realms teachings to assist you in discovering these talents and gifts. (If you are not aware of yours now consider: The Angel News Network's Life Mastery program). Your gifts and talents are 'soul qualities' you can joyfully share with the world. They are not necessarily a job or career (but can be). Your talents and gifts come through you with Divine Grace and ease empowered by you following your bliss. Because these soul qualities are an essential/innate part of your soul plan, they come to you effortlessly, and even though others may have somewhat similar qualities, yours are uniquely yours to share in world service.

In regard to your individuated soul plan in this life, remember, you are unique, since no other has the experiences and relationship you do. Where your unique integration of talents and gifts intersects with the needs of others or the world, you become the unique solution to that need, as only you can be and do. As you reach out to (world) serve others' needs you further activate your soul plan. **As in all Creation, this is the balance of giving and receiving that powers all life and the universe. THIS GIVES MEANING TO LIFE**. You stop the struggle to survive life by becoming life itself. You enter a spiritual ascension adventure story of self- discovery through self-mastery (knowing who you are and why you are here).

As your sciences and spiritual truths further merge, you become aware that a higher realm power is running things, and it is your joy that further fuels the journey. In your vernacular, *you go with the flow*. You become the moment where there is no time or distance, only now, and things become effortless through self-confidence, intuitiveness, and self -love. You feel you are where you are supposed to be, doing what you were meant to do. You discover complete meaning, value and purpose in life in that moment. This 'flow' allows self-empowerment while interfacing with the physical world. You lose the sense of separation/duality of self and gain a true sense of self with the physical world; **you become one** by being in the now.

You are beginning to realize that the **meaning of life** is not just a journey of personal ego fulfillment (although this can be temporarily satisfying) but a fuller soul plan activation that allows service to others and your world as a measure of the growth and expansion of your own soul. Actually, the desire to serve the needs of others can activate/stimulate sleeping talents and gifts within self. Your soul knows that it serves a grander meaning to be in service to others as your man power evolves into God Power. The portal to higher consciousness and personal processed growth is a cosmic choreography in which you are all supporting and loving one another. This is you becoming the Creator through the Christ Consciousness energies of loving one another (remember that teaching?).

Your entire life's journey is the meaning and mission of your life; realizing life is a constant personal process (not an end result) within this dimension, by allowing your BEingness to be reflected within your doingness. When this lifetime is complete, it will not be what you did but how and why you did it (BEingness) through your compassion and caring for self and others that refines and defines your eternal soul.

Remember that **the meaning of life and your soul plan is an ongoing laboratory of learning (Love)** until you finally intersect with your Divinity, and the two become one. The meaning of life is a remarkable template/blueprint for you to discover who you are and why you are here **by fully knowing your talents and gifts and how to serve others through them**, thus allowing both growth and expansion beyond measure and meaning of the human mind.

DIVINE DISCUSSIONS

The Returning Of Oneness

From: Council Of The Galactic Federations (GF).

Dear Brothers And Sisters Of Planet Earth, Milky Way Galaxy,

We of the Council of The Galactic Federations (GF) come to you at this soul activation epoch of your planet, affecting each human and all soul plans within and upon the planet, in like kind. This is a divine moment within the creation of your planet and yourselves to shape-shift and **return to your true BEingness of Light, the transmitter of Love, through Oneness.**

Through Divine Consciousness, as each planet is chosen to be created it is embedded with a soul plan, a purpose in being. In your case, that purpose is to know and apply the energy of Cosmic Love. Your human feelings of love are a minute reflection of the universal powers and purpose of Love as the building block of Creation. Love is the highest frequency of existence; thus, in turn, it is capable of constructing everything. When Love is not applied you have destruction.

We of GF, in concert with the twelve star systems who agreed to seed your planet hundreds of millions of years ago (long before you came), intended your planet to be a Divine Experiment (which you eventually signed onto). Various Star and Galactic councils agreed that the mandate of freedom of choice and will would be essential for this planetary experiment/evolution to be successful. There have been moments where this mandate has been most challenging, as you have experienced throughout your human history. But since the purpose of your planet is to experience every aspect of Creation, we knew it could not be otherwise. Coming from Light into density and returning to Light is a mighty preparation for self-mastery and service to not only your world but worlds beyond. This is the choice you all made prior to coming here.

All of Creation is 'governed' by various planetary, solar system, galaxy, star systems and universal and multiverse councils. Your planet has been protected through many of these councils throughout the eons. The true creation and history of the human species will be made known to you (see page 4). Some of the founding principles of the United States of America reflect these various councils. Thus far, your world has not maintained and sustained the principles of Oneness necessary for all this to be revealed to you. This will happen. How and when this will be achieved is through your freedom of choice and will.

Each of the twelve star systems (some remain unknown to you) brought an intention into your creation. They represent the highest intention of each system. The channel we are coming through at this time has recently received from Adama, residing in your Inner Earth Civilization of Lemuria, a *Sacred Trilogy Of Teachings*, which contains the majority of the twelve Star System intentions. These are available to you (see pages 168-192) through the endeavor known as *The Angel News Network* whose mission is to bring higher realm messages, such as this one, to humanity in order to increase your frequency/consciousness so all of which we speak may further be known to you.

Very little of the true creation of your planet and yourselves is known or remembered at this time. This is about to change through the planetary soul activations by various surface energetic vortices/portals openings throughout your planet. Originally uploaded into the core of your planet during its creation were the codes necessary to activate what is taking place at present. Various surface vortices/portals are opened (as below, so above) as these active codes move upward. These vortices/portals then create an energetic network across the entire planet healing the cause and effect of your duality and confrontation (an essential aspect of your learning process). Recently, some brethren of this endeavor called *The Angel News Network* were chosen to be proxies for humanity at the central vortex known as Mount Shasta to perform sacred rituals to facilitate the opening of these various vortices/portals. Documentation of a chronicle of these rituals was assigned to this channel so that all who read them may become proxies themselves (See *Coming Home To Lemuria, An Ascension Adventure Story*.) As many of you are being taught, your evolution is an individuated process of inside out since each of you is returning to your Divine Light Body, along with the planet herself. Since planet Earth and humanity are created of the same Cosmic elements, this process is called **The Returning Of Oneness**, or as the Archangelic Realms in service to humanity have said, **The World Of One Way**, showing galactic, universal and multiverse Oneness.

This 'Oneness' is coming about through your experiencing all the duality you have so that you never return to that duality again within your service to your world and beyond. This is how you have chosen to learn and master yourselves (a reflection of Creation) to become the master teachers, Ascended Masters of all you serve and beyond.

Since your planet and you are aspects of twelve star systems and their numerous solar systems and planets, you have been influenced many times throughout your evolutionary pathway by various advanced civilizations. The true history of all this is forthcoming as you ready yourselves to receive it. Civilizations such as Lemuria and Atlantis and others currently predate your accepted known written history. But when you arrive at what remains of ancient Egypt, Mayan and Aztec civilizations you have many unanswered questions about 'how'. Your journey has been one of contraction (pulling back) and expansion (connecting to higher realms). Your connection to higher realms has made all of your advancement possible (building golden ages). The advancement has not always been a straight line forward through your gifted free will. But this Cosmic choreography is surely moving you forward through waking up.

All that precedes your awareness now has had various positive and negative effects through your freedom of will and choice journey. The time-line on this is coming to an end now as a result of this final 2,000-year epoch of your planet and your human destiny to return to Light. As many know, you are moving from your carbon-based density back to Light, the transmitter of Cosmic Love (the foundation of Creation). The true frequency science of Love will be known to you. All this is a reflection of the Ascension Process of the planet herself. As the planet returns to Light all within and upon her body will do so as well or be given the opportunity to ascend elsewhere.

We have been meeting with your world governments and religious leaders for thousands of years to assist them without interfering. In order to maintain control they have never shared such encounters. The game changer will be for all of humanity to know we and other worlds exist. You might ask why this has not already happened. The answer is you were not ready to accept the wisdom and the stewardship of the power of Creation.

Your world is still in the process of mastering the ONENESS of yourselves. This is an essential aspect of we revealing ourselves to you and you moving forward. Many teachings are again flooding into humanity from higher realms to assist in the process of mastering self and creating communities of equality, harmony and balance, thus Oneness. By looking at your world you can see there is much to be accomplished.

Beloved brothers and sisters of planet Earth, this brief message of Truth, Love and Light may bring up more questions than answers. We ask that you surrender to not knowing all at this time. In the not knowing you will allow your readiness to know all the wonders of the universe. You are being given the foundation of all you are able to integrate and apply for the good of all at this time.

More of you than ever before have chosen to be here at this grand evolution and destination from whence you came: Love and Light through Oneness.

Soon we shall meet.

The Year Of The Starseed, 2016

From: Archangel Uriel, World Teacher And Guardian.

As many of you know, beautiful planet Earth was 'seeded' by twelve different star systems bringing the highest qualities of each star system into the Earthly plane. Earth is a grand experiment of learning to love, the 'Lover-versity' of the Universe. At present, planet Earth is within the final 2,000-year cycle (beginning 2012) to ascend into a higher state of vibration -- thus consciousness. It is humanity's Divine Destiny to evolve into 'We Consciousness' in order to create a new world paradigm of equality, harmony and balance. This is a personal process of inside out, not outside in. No matter how the outside world may appear in upheaval and chaos (clearing and cleansing), this Ascension Process is taking place for those who choose it through their freedom of choice and will by healing the relationship with Self -- Self-reflecting *All There Is*.

The year 2016 began within an unprecedented force of higher realm star energies to support the above process. Now within every month, each of the twelve star systems that seeded the planet will be firmly present to support the Ascension Process of humanity further. This message is a recap of the first two months January and February, followed by other months and their respected star systems as the year unfolds and star energies further integrate. We shall monthly review star systems such as Arcturian, Lyran, Bootes, Orion, Aquarius, Andromeda and some as yet unknown systems. We shall review each month as it is revealed from the higher realms perspective. Before we begin by starseeding January and February, let us briefly discuss what being a human starseed and light worker/way shower means.

Starseeds are those humans who presently reside on planet Earth but know within their higher self that their origins are not from this planet. Starseeds often have a connection with the star world from whence they came. Light workers/way showers are those that tend to be starseeds on earth whose soul plan includes (through their talents and gifts) accomplishing higher good work of the *Universal Infinite Intelligence*. They spread applied knowledge into wisdom and acceptance of the innate positive powers of humans and that of other higher realms.

Light worker's/way shower's are most often starseeds due to their inherent need to find the positive powers of the Universe and share them. This allows teachings of the powers that manifest eternal good. The light workers/way showers main mission is to teach others that there are different forces than those of the current density of humanity. They know the present state of humanity is a teaching tool, allowing humanity to evolve/ascend/transmute into a higher state of being.

So those who know they are starseeds will, or are, gravitating towards teaching Universal Truths of the light worker/way shower, intending the betterment of humanity until humanity unites/ascends into Oneness with the star worlds from whence they came.

These monthly descriptions present a brief explanation of what is happening and why without an overload of information. For those who wish to have more information about the star systems know that it is available through your cyberspace, a gift from the Archangelic Realm of Uriel.

January/Sirius
The first two weeks of the New Year, creating the new

you and world, filled with the Sirius star energies. Sirius is the brightest star within Earth's heavens and is often called the "Stargate" of the world since it has always played a major role in earth's evolutionary and galactic history. Many past advanced civilizations such as Lemurian, Atlantean or Egyptian contained crystal/vibrational energy from Sirius. These energies brought social structure and wisdom that allowed the construction of powerful electro-magnetic energy plants such as the great pyramids throughout the planet. These assertive energies, to effect change, were strongly felt throughout humanity's emotional, mental and physical bodies the entire month of January.

February/Pleiadian
The assertive Sirius energies began to lift in February as the gentler Pleiadian energies arrived in February (the month of love), allowing the human believing mental body to move more into service to the knowing heart. The Pleiadian energies have perfected the expression of unconditional love and equality, balance and harmony, reflecting within self and out picturing into society as a whole. These energies allow the balance of the emotional, mental and physical bodies transmuting into multi-dimensionality. This energy is more feminine while the Sirius energy is more masculine. The peace and sharing focus of this energy is all about healing the past and present, allowing focus on the present. The presence of this energy and all other star energies throughout this year is facilitating the genetic transmutation of the human DNA and chakras from carbon based reality to crystalline light.

March/Arcturian
As the planet begins its out breath towards Spring

(winter is an in breath), and the ascension lei lines of the planet further connect, we now move into the Arcturian star energy gateway, through which humans pass during death and re-birth. These star energies function as a way station, from non-physical consciousness, to become accustomed to physicality. The Arcturians teach us the most fundamental ingredient for living in a fifth dimension is LOVE. These Star Beings are very powerful healers and assist us in balancing our emotional, mental and physical bodies. This healing allows our further connection to our higher selves and higher realms achieving self-mastery.

April/Sirius (revisited)
Now that you have completed the first quarter of your unprecedented year 2016 you are revisiting your Stargate energies of Sirius (January) in order to better live in the present moment. January also represented a combination of all the past Golden Ages you have experienced (Lemurian, Atlantean, Egyptian, Greek, Aztec, Man, Hopi, etc.) allowing surrender-ship to the unknown. April will begin a step by step process of balancing the masculine assertive energy with the receptive feminine energy that brings the spiritual and physical into existence within this frequency, thus allowing a balance of giving and receiving in your world. It is time, if you so choose to surrender to not knowing where all the probabilities and possibilities of creation live. This allows the death of the old and the birthing of the new you and new paradigm of equality, harmony and balance. You are beginning to see and know the 'self' is a reflection of *All There Is*.

Note: Follow the complete teaching on PhillipEltonCollins.com and The AngelNewsNetwork.com.

Twelve Codes Of Consciousness

From: I AM Presence and Christ Consciousness Energies.

Dear Beloved Children Of Earth,

You are completely conscious (awakened) when you are able to apply these *Twelve Codes of Consciousness* gifted from the twelve Star Systems, which seeded your planet:

1. **Allowing** manifestation/creation to happen without attempting to control or own its outcome.

2. **Feeling** joyful/blissful for no apparent reason at all; allowing others to entrain to this higher frequency.

3. **Knowing** and seeing the integration of all things upon and within this planet.

4. **Being** filled with gratitude, allowing abundance by focusing upon what is.

5. **'Thinking'** with your hearts, allowing synchronistic and spontaneous experiences.

6. **Being** versus doing, allowing being to create doing.

7. **Letting** go of all negative emotions creating imbalances, dis-ease and death.

8. **Knowing** there is no separation, duality, thus conflict.

9. **Letting** go of the need to explain the actions of others, knowing it is a chosen learning process.

10. **Loving** unconditionally, not giving to get.

11. **Being** directly connected to the higher realms that maintain, sustain and evolve all life.

12. **Knowing** that Love is the foundation of all and knowing how to apply it.

When you master these, dear Children, you shall be free from yourselves and united in Oneness, your Divine Destiny.

Alphabetical Listing Of Articles: W

What Does New Mean?
Why Is Truth Important?
Wondrous Ways Of Light Workers/Way
Showers: A Divine Discussion

What Does New Mean?

From: Archangel Uriel, World Teacher And Guardian.

Beloved, Choosing To Be Human,

As the New Year begins, once again humanity is given the opportunity to create something new within individual lives and the world. What exactly does 'being new' mean, dear ones?

As human, you are constantly being given the divine choice to create newness within each moment of the now. Your body is creating new cells each moment, in fact, new bodies each year. You are gifted with the opportunity to constantly make another choice based upon past choices each moment. The newness you create is the pathway to your Divinity, dear ones. Without the choices of creating new you cannot advance into your eternal pathway of being in service to *All There Is*.

What and how you create this 'newness' within your freedom of choice and will is based upon your ability to apply wisdom (applied knowledge) of what has worked in past lives, past moments in this lifetime and at present. Many of you are still in a personal process of learning how to master the choices you make as a result of the relationship with self, thus others. We of the Archangelic Realms are gifting you with many tools to remind you how to advance from old to new. This is simply how you have chosen to learn by choosing to be human. And yes, dear ones, you all made the decision to be human and learn by being human.

The task is can you accept with compassion, thus forgive, how and why you have chosen to learn the way you have chosen? In fact, the way you have chosen to create the new you (in a new year) is the only way you can master what it is you need to learn.

So newness is another gift from Creation reminding you that you are the creator creating the new. The old is the tool to show you what works and what does not, if you choose to apply it. This aspect of old to new is a major hang-up for humanity right now and is causing much of your pain moving into suffering. Your mental bodies are often stuck in the old as a comfort zone refusing to apply knowledge into wisdom. You would rather suffer than move into the newness of the unknown. This is a form of insanity waiting to cease. Your world reflects this greatly until you have had enough of the madness and choose to make another choice into the new, knowing the old no longer works. Again, being human (human being), this is the choice you have chosen from which to learn.

There is an easier, simpler way to learn. Are you ready to apply it? This comes from accepting the new with grace and ease as an essential aspect of your evolutionary path. You and the universe are constantly creating the new. There is nothing else but the creation of new going on all around you. Your resistance to the new is what often scares you and creates what you are experiencing now in your lives and world.

Accepting the new also has another component as well, dear ones. Can you accept you are not in control of what you have not created? That includes you and your world. The human mental body, as a fear response, has created the illusion (the ego defense) that you are in control of yourself and your world. You are not, dear ones. And you are not because you have not yet learned to love yourselves and world enough to be in control of anything.

You are in the process of creating the new you and world now to remember there are higher realms and forces from whence you came who are the factors maintaining and sustaining your lives and world. In fact, these forces created all your past advanced golden ages and the one you are attempting to create as your final one now...through newness. The newness is your eternal connection to these higher realms of Creation, allowing you to be the creator creating. Your destiny is through your newness; you and we higher realms become one.

Dear humans, you have had many, many lifetimes upon this planet to arrive at this moment of the new you. The new you is the eternal you that has no beginning and no end. New can never begin or end; it just is, as you are. Please place your hands upon your hearts and repeat after us, "I AM New." Through the new you, you can and will create communities of equality, harmony and balance. Through the new you, you will come to know you are created from Love, you are Love, you are loved, and you are lovable. This is the reason and meaning of new, dear ones.

Happy New You New Year.

Why Is Truth Important?

From: Phillip Elton Collins.

Throughout my training as a Light Ascension Therapist, continuing to teach what I need to learn, and throughout the many books I have read and written, I have remained fascinated with the meaning, value and purpose of truth and the lack of it in our world today. How did things get this way, and how can we as a human species make another choice through our free will? And what exactly is 'truth' anyway since we seem to have such a short supply of it?

Joining many higher realms, I directly accessed myself, and reflecting the teachings and tools of many others, began a *Divine Discussion* (Visit PhillipEltonCollins.com and look under the EVENTS tab for information, including audio files of past gatherings.) on truth, and/or the lack of it.

God's Glossary, A Divine Dictionary, Definitions To Change Everything, defines 'truth' as: "Something that radiates from the knowing heart, realizing beliefs come from the mind and can change. Truth is inclusive, embracing *All There Is* in an eternal cosmic dance that is complete. Truth sets us free to be who we are and to know why we are here. Truth is constant and cannot be destroyed. Untruth is a creation of humanity, an illusion of the 3D reality that has kept us trapped in duality, lack and limitation far too long."

Perhaps it is time for humanity to make another choice in creating a **constant contact of truth** in our lives. So why is truth not an every moment reality, and how did untruth gain such a foothold, and how can we achieve more truth to finally set us free from ourselves and others??

In my heart I know the reason that so many higher realms are constantly connecting with humanity is so we can understand ourselves more fully to eventually free ourselves from ourselves in order to embrace and become our Eternal Spiritual BEings (a form of learning of which we agreed). Much of the teaching that my colleagues, Joel Anastasi and Jeff Fasano, and I, at The Angel News Network directly receive from higher realms has to do with *who we are and why we are here.*

Most people do not remember what they came here to achieve, not fully knowing their talents and gifts. We are here to activate our Divine Soul Plans (reason to be here). See *Activate Your Soul Plan: Angel Answers & Actions*, in the Angel News Network library. The most essential thing forgotten is that **we are powerful spiritual beings choosing to have this human experience,** and we can directly connect with the higher realms from whence we came anytime we intend. Another one of the many self-empowering publications at The Angel News Network is *Life Mastery, A Guide For Creating The Life You Want And The Courage To Live It.* This is a teaching from Archangel Michael, which creates a dialogue and exercises to address the truth of you.

Once you know the 'who' and the 'why' of your life as a foundation you can build the what, how, when and where. But many do not know these teachings and are accepting the present way of their lives and world (even though their heart hurts for more). They have convinced themselves that 'surviving' life each day is enough, that lies are part of life and killing one another in war is acceptable human behavior.

What we have not fully realized is that often our personal lives and our erroneous beliefs are sustained by the untruths and fears of others. Thus, few of us are able to maneuver through the upheaval of life on Planet Earth, and those of us who do know are often shunned, not believed, or killed. But many of us, who do know, continue to follow our resonance and discernment (our internal gyro system) as an essential aspect of our Divine Soul Plans, our purpose in being here. We do not concern ourselves with those who believe or disbelieve us or how many show up to read or listen to what we have to say. We simply tell the truth supported by the higher realms from whence we came.

Of course, one of the largest variables is how to reveal the truth to many who are not ready to know it. We are constantly intending that we can 'strike a chord' within their souls or hearts where they might hear something that can become their own truth. As messengers of self-empowerment and truth, we understand many people have no desire to change, and change will not most likely take place in this lifetime. Then we accept with compassion, forgive and move on. We know in our hearts that necessary changes in life are going to take place (a process of inside out, not outside in) no matter what or who chooses it.

This truth we shall hold: We are not here to convince nor to control what we did not create but to reveal the truth and allow others to decide for themselves their truth (through their freedom of will and choice). Higher realms have taught us that humanity slices up into three portions: (1) one-third is here to know the truth and effect a change from the old to new, creating equality, harmony and balance, (2) One-third is in resistance to any change or the truth being revealed, and (3) the final one-third has no idea what is going on. Those resonating with this writing are of the first one-third.

Many people are not able to change due to a lack of trust. Throughout our pre-and recorded histories and past and present lives, there have been many situations when humanity was lied to and controlled by others whose primary objective was power and control (attempting to control what we have not created is a grand folly of humanity's wounded ego). When some of us tried to reveal the truth we were often (as mentioned earlier) not believed or sometimes killed. This created a fear, locked into our cellular memory, which propagated onto future lives through our spiritual DNA. Fear is an absence of Love, and healing that lack of Love is essential within our evolutionary personal process of ascension. The Angel News Network (TheAngelNewsNetwork.com) offers many tools in healing your relationship with self that affects your relationship with others and the world.

Those of us who live our lives through soulful **resonance** (how we feel about it from our hearts) and **discernment** (how we think about it from our minds), rather than the beliefs and truths of others, may be seen as threats. But through freedom of will and choice we become the ones to effect the needed change within our weary world. Without us, there would be no change.

Freed thinkers know we cannot hide our emotions, thoughts and truth. We know the non-truthful work secretively, through deceit and denial of their deceit, and those untruthful people will see *us of truth* as untrustworthy, as we do them.

Still, at present, many people continue to live in fear of telling the truth because they have been or can be threatened by controlling/manipulating others who need secrets kept or insist upon others adopting rigid belief system(s). Does this sound familiar? Only a healed, strong, loving relationship with self will allow you to break through attempted control. Remember, humanity cannot control what it did not create, and others did not create you!

Let us remember that even our silence, *by not speaking the truth when we know it,* supports the untruth. Fear of speaking the truth has also allowed some to create reasons why it is acceptable to tell a non-truth. Some non-truth tellers even can reach a point in believing their own non-truth, which can lead to greater and greater non-truths. Eventually those around these people no longer believe them even when they are telling the truth. Gaining future trust will be a lengthy process or not achieved at all.

All of our relationships with self-mirroring to others are founded upon love of self, trust and the compassion we have for self and each other. Lack of trust, due to a lack of Love, has created all the negative personal and world relationships we are experiencing at present. These lacks affect our soul and us emotionally, mentally and physically. Through knowing and honoring our truth (who we are and why we are here), our needs (do you know your needs?) and our boundaries (what are yours?) and those of others, we can create the world we say we want. **Knowing your truth, needs and boundaries are essential** to knowing and sharing your truth. We at The Angel News Network are here to support you in knowing and applying these. Honor your own truth, needs and boundaries and those of others. If it's time to leave a non-resonating/non-discerning relationship, do so, and allow another choice to come through.

If we intend to be in any successful relationship (be it personal or globally) it needs to be based upon truth. This is the reason we have so many divorces, and our domestic and world governments are often at each other's throats. There is no trust due to past untruthful behavior. When untruths and half-truths are historically and repeatedly exchanged, it makes it impossible to know the truth when it is told. Many world leaders have simply lost the ability to trust other leaders after years of non-truths. Now it's usually the one who waves the biggest sword who gets the most media attention, but even that no longer works so much if both have nuclear power and can destroy each other, along with millions of others and the planet. This has happened with past advanced civilizations, and it was not very effective! **Until truth becomes the Code of Conduct worldwide, the world will not be at peace.** Who wrote, "The truth will set us free?"

So the question becomes, "Is it possible to reintroduce truth and trust into our relationships?" **Not everyone is untruthful.** Plenty of conscious, caring people understand and apply the importance of truth and trust in many of their personal, professional and governmental relationships. Let us come together and build communities of equality, harmony and balance. It is time, if we so choose, for we the people, by the people, for the people to stand up and be counted and insist on selecting partners and leaders with the same wisdom about truth.

It is time to move beyond the past and present and to accept with compassion and forgive this *untruthful* way of learning what we need to learn as a human species and begin to choose truth throughout our lives. The need and desire for world peace and successful relationships is awakening as we awaken as human beings. Endeavors such as The Angel News Network are dedicated to you and me finding the peace within so that we can activate a process of inside out (not outside in) into the world.

Perhaps it is time to remember we are all of the same Cosmic elements, created from the same Oneness. We all need the same things to be loved and safe. There is plenty for all without the few attempting to control the many through duality, confrontation and non-truths. Let us further shift our awareness into Oneness/We Consciousness where we know we are creating within the Oneness of *All There Is*.

My intention in writing this is that we be able to awaken, to know who we are and why we are here, speaking our truth freely and insisting that others do the same. The truth begins with each one of us reflecting out to others....

Please know we of The Angel News Network are here to support you within your personal process and being the truth.

The Light of Truth never fails.

Wondrous Ways Of Light Workers/Way Showers: A Divine Discussion

From: Archangels Gabriel, Michael, Raphael and Uriel.

Note: This channel occurred in preparation for a *Divine Discussions* gathering.

You are all light workers to a greater or lesser extent. It merely depends upon your bent. You all have a Divine Soul Plan, (mission and purpose in this lifetime) and come here possessing various healing modalities. And if you so choose, it is time to release, not conceal, and reveal your various healing modalities, revealing your true realities. There is no way to lose.

You may partake in your modalities any way you choose. For example, you may choose to work with individuals as a bio-energetic healer. That may be your mission and purpose working as a healer with individuals or groups.

Some may work with individuals or groups in certain techniques, and that remains your mission and purpose being quite complete.

Way showers are the light workers who bring their gifts and talents out into the world in a larger way. That is their pay. A way shower shows the way for others to move onto their path to create a new world of community, harmony, equality and balance with no set path. Way showers may choose to work in different ways. Some may choose to work with individuals as healers. Some may choose to take their gifts and talents further on the path into the unknown than others in service to the masses.

We ask you to ask yourself, "Am I a light worker? Am I a way shower? Am I both?"

It is time for you to begin to define specifically why you are here. Some may be able to do this now. Some will be able to answer as they continue on their life journey and discover their purpose in this lifetime. It is important to know your life purpose. It will be defined and refined as you continue on your life journey. Prepare for your life to change. Some of you may choose to remain where you are, and some will choose to go further. Your path will unfold as you take each step forward.

If you are ready, steady yourself and let's see what being a light worker and way shower can be:

The light worker and way shower knows how to surrender to not knowing, allowing a trust of the unknown. Within the unknown, escaping the human mind, all probabilities and possibilities of truth come through. Light workers and way showers know and trust that the void of the universe fills with consciousness to support themselves and others, allowing intuition and wisdom (applied knowledge) to be applied.

When working with others, light workers and way showers do not have to tell you all they know and how they can heal you. They are there to allow you to receive what it is that you are ready to receive, allowing an organic balance of giving and receiving. They know that healing is a process of inside out, not outside in. And that they are there to assist you in healing you.

Maintaining and sustaining the self-empowerment of others is an essential process of the true light worker and way shower. They are not here to fix you. They are present to assist in awakening the innate powers within others through a relationship of equality, harmony and balance.

Learning to 'think' with the knowing heart and allowing the believing mental body to gently move back into the service of the heart is crucial for the light worker and way shower. They know the heart has downloaded within its DNA all the data needed to assist another within their healing. This way the ego, housed within the mental body, does not have to know it all, be in control or be right.

Releasing all judgment, shaming or blaming about a situation is key for the light worker and way shower. They know that everything has simply been a way that they, or another, chose to learn the way they needed to learn, the way they needed to learn it. This includes 'accidents,' disease and death.

Allowing another to be heard is essential to any healing process for the light worker and way shower. Creating a space and relationship of safety and sanctuary is vital. Within this environment, there is no right or wrong or who is in control. Allowing ownership of what has been created, thus releasing victimhood, excels the healing process. Sometimes just showing up is all that is needed.

Through humility and compassion the light worker and way shower offer support through the resonance (how one feels) and discernment (how one thinks) of the other. This way another can make a decision different from the light worker and way shower, allowing the support of the highest good for all.

The light worker and way shower know that feeling all emotions is essential. They know the basis for physical imbalances are the emotions creating blocked energy flows within the physical body. Once the emotions are fully felt, they can be released and balance restored.

Staying connected to the higher realms from whence we came and who love and support us is the most essential aspect of being a light worker and way shower.

Finally, the light worker and way shower have taken a Cosmic conscious oath to be in personal and collective service to others and the world.

Phillip's Conclusion: Which are you a light worker or way shower or both? It is my intention to draw our attention to the *wondrous ways of the light workers and way showers* that allow us to be the most divine and best we can be.

The Angel News Network offers many tools to help you discover who you are and why you are here. As you work with this material, you will discover your purpose and your passion, and you will realize that you are here for world service. World service is about bringing your gifts and talents into the world in a way that brings you joy. In doing so, you are choosing to be a light worker and a way shower.

Alphabetical Listing Of Articles: Y

Your Cosmic Mother: At The Valentine Vortex Of Love
Your Star, Your Sun, Your Destiny

Your Cosmic Mother At The Valentine Vortex Of Love

From: Cosmic Mother.

Dear Beloved Children, Being So Human,

For many eons, your world has been ruled and seemingly controlled by the masculine energy, assertive energy, chosen to largely diminish feminine energy, the receptive energy. At this crucial time of your planetary and human species Ascension Process, we would like to introduce ourselves to many of you. **We are your Cosmic Mother** responsible to the planetary logos forces which maintain and sustain your planet. We are here to assist you in balancing the masculine and feminine energies, which is a vital balancing that needs to take place in order for you to evolve into your Oneness and Divinity. Let us further explain how and why this is taking place.

Dear Children still often attempting to control one another, your reason to be here (your 'golden goal'), your primary purpose in being on this planet, is to learn to love self, one another, in order to be in world service.

Through balancing these two vital masculine and feminine cosmic energies and committing to spiritual growth as a life priority, you can and will achieve *Love Incarnate*. When the masculine and feminine energies balance, they create a **vibration of consciousness,** which can levitate and manifest equality, harmony and balance. The basis of your duality, separation and confrontation at present is the result of the imbalance of these forces of creation. Have you learned enough from the absence of this balance to accept your Divinity at this time?

Your Cosmic Mother consciousness/energy expresses itself in freedom, equality and liberty for all life on this planet. We have come to you many times in the past through the 'Mary Energies' expressed in your goddesses, spiritual leaders and deities within many of your religious and spiritual doctrines. An essential way to connect with us now is through your knowing and loving heart; begin *to think* with your heart, as your believing mental body moves back into service to your knowing heart. Your heart has stored within its DNA, from all lifetimes, all the wisdom you need to embrace your Cosmic Mother and create the life you say you want, one of unity. We are not suggesting eliminating the mostly masculine mental body; we are speaking of balance, which the universal laws of Creation require. As you look at your world, you can easily see the lack of balance preventing equality and harmony. What we speak of is the core issue, an essential aspect that needs to shift in order to move forward.

When the energies of freedom, equality and liberty are lovingly expressed individually within enough of humanity to create a quantum shift, the entire vibration of the planet and humanity will rise to a level where the atoms and electrons within your physical bodies will speed up (matching that of the planet), allowing you to evolve into your immortality and Divinity. Disease, aging and death will become a thing of the past. **So, is it worth it to now begin to 'listen to your mother', your Cosmic Mother?**

You can and will, if you so choose, join the Ascended

Masters, the Angelic Realms, Inner Earth Civilizations, the Star Systems that seeded your planet and other higher hosts through something called the magnetic Law Of Attraction (what you focus on through your emotions and thoughts you create). You are the Creator creating, you know? How, what, and when you create expresses through your freedoms of choice and will and activation of your Divine Soul Plans. We cannot and will not do it for you.

As you fully **focus your attention on your intention** and lubricate the process with love (your reason to be here), you manifest into your life and world what it is you say you want: equality, harmony and balance. Bring your higher self, your I AM Presence, your Christ Consciousness (call it what you will) into the process. This will bring an electromagnetic energy into the process, like sticking a plug into an electric outlet.

Here's another suggestion from your Cosmic Mother to assist you: Find a comfortable chair, seat yourself with your feet firmly connected to the floor (the Earth), and take a series of deep breaths to center yourself. Visualize an electromagnetic energy (you can see it as light or a sound or both), integrating throughout your entire physical body, emotionally and mentally. Allow this to happen for several minutes, morning, noon and night. You will be surprised and delighted how you feel and how differently you see life.

Dear Children, we know and understand how many of you feel, and what you are experiencing, which is a final clearing and cleansing of your planet and selves. We ask that you not be discouraged. We are simply *showing* you the light at the end of the tunnel and further allowing you to have a fuller understanding of your evolution process. **You Are Evolving**, incarnating into Love, no matter how things look outside of yourselves. Your Ascension Process is one of inside out, not outside in. What you maintain and sustain inside you is vital. You actually signed on to this 'human contract', and your Cosmic Mother intends to teach, love and support you all the way. Again, this is a personal process you chose to do yourself, and your mother, nor no one else, can do it for you.

Remember, Divine Children of planet Earth, the 'Lover-versity' of Love, Love is the frequency and foundation of all Creation, functioning in equality, harmony and balance. Love is the holistic healer. Love is life. Love is the Cosmic Substance Of Light out of which all is created. You are learning that enough Love can transmute, transform, transition anything (including the world you are experiencing now). Mother Love is one of the purest expressions of Love. We intend for you to know you came from this Love, you are loved, you are lovable, and you are destined to eternally live in Love.

In closing, your Cosmic Mother asks that you bring from your loving hearts, into your world, a compassion for self and one another, an attitude of gratitude (for what is in your lives rather than what is not), to honor, to do no harm to your planet and human bodies (as one) and to further allow wisdom to come from higher realms....

Your Loving Cosmic Mother knows your best is yet to be.

Your Star, Your Sun, Your Destiny

From: Cosmic Keepers of Creation.

Dear Human Star Seeds,

Many *Creator Consultants such as* we *Cosmic Keepers of Creation* came together to create your planet Earth. We gifted you with a teaching on how the earth was created (see "A New Creation Story" on page 4). You may refer to that, if it resonates for you. What is not in that previous message is that **your planet was created by twelve star systems** (twelve suns) coming together to give the best of themselves in the creation of your home planet. *So, in effect, you are all Star Beings from various worlds.* Each of you has a primary star system from which you originated. You can learn what system you originally came from and learn more about the mission of that star system, if you wish. You have named many of your constellations from these stellar homes.

When you look up into your night sky and see so many stars/suns we wish for you to know that **they, too, went through an Ascension Process very much like the one you are going through now.** They began as a planet and **transmuted back into a body of Light** from whence they came. This is the process you and your planet are evolving into at this unique time of ascension (**moving to a higher frequency/consciousness of existence**). This is the Divine Destiny of all worlds. You are within the process of **transitioning from a carbon-based reality to one of Light.** Love and Light are the building blocks of all Creation and you are in an ascension of becoming Love and Light (again). Then, through your freedom of will and choice you can decide what happens next, since creation is a never-ending, expanding growth.

In order to maintain and sustain life upon and within your new *Light world,* you also will be of a Light vibration the same as your home planet, or you will not be here. Those who choose not to transmute into Light during this final 2,000-year cycle of your planet will be given the opportunity to do so within another galaxy and planet. Do not worry. There is no rush. You will all arrive at the same Divine Light destination; it's just a matter of how and when for each of you. But we shall ask you, "What are you choosing at this time?"

The above information may or may not be new to you. For those for whom this is an introduction, please know further information is available to you by simply asking. You are all within the process of becoming multi-dimensional, so you can have direct access to all dimensions and any process or information needed. Dear Star Beings, all wisdom about your creation is available to you. The forces that created you and your world are forces of Love and never intend anything but Love for you! As you approach a new year within your Earth cycle of ascension, please know you came from Love, are loved and are lovable.

An unhealed relationship with self, based upon fear, doubt and ignorance has prevented your advancement and can continue to do so. Many higher realms are coming together at this unique time to garner the tools and teachings necessary to help you achieve your ascension success. We are teaching you how to access and 'think,' with your all-knowing hearts, allowing your minds to move back into service to your hearts. Everything you need to know is stored within the DNA of your hearts and has been passed on from lifetime to lifetime. It's all about **healing any aspects of self** that prevent you from surrendering and trusting your ability to be and do this. You will continue to be within a personal process as long as you reside within the dimension in which you currently live. *For many, it is your sabotaging mental body through the allowed manipulations of others that has set back your Ascension Process many times in the past.* This will not be allowed much longer this time around since you are within the final 2000-year cycle of ascension for this particular planet.

Please know none of these teachings came from the human mind. These teachings come from higher realms that know the human mind only too well and have transcended it. The human mind has been of great service to your evolution, but it is time to gain a higher perspective within your process.

Let us briefly discuss your sun, your star, since it is your destiny to live upon or within one.

Actually, you have very little knowledge or truth about your sun. Most 'knowledge' about the sun reflects your relationship with self, often based on fear, doubt and ignorance. *So let us shed some light on your sun.*

Nothing about your sun can harm you if common sense is applied. Sun storms and flares will not affect your health or communications systems. Why would Creation, who created you from Love, harm your life in any way? The sun, also the one that is being created as your new home, is a conscious sentient being and has no intention to harm. Suns are created to support life, not harm nor destroy it. Destructive behavior is the folly of humanity, not the forces of Creation. Your unnecessary or made up fears do not serve your highest good. Since humanity cannot change activities of the sun, and your continuous monitoring of the sun's ever-active solar activity has brought forth little understanding, perhaps it is time to surrender and know that all sun life is life affirming.

As you know, without suns there can be no life. That includes your planet. Since the sun is a powerful *planetary body,* it is very active. Much of its activity (solar winds, flares, storms) within its own magnetic field, are the ways the sun expresses Love from whence it came. These natural solar activities change like your seasons. Your scientists really do not understand the true reasons for the changes, so they often negatively project what they 'think' they are and how they may affect the Earth (which is often incorrect). **When you transcend into your Light body living on a star, all the wisdom you need will be given to you.**

As mentioned earlier, many mighty forces came together to create your planet and your sun around which you revolve. These forces, through conscious Cosmic science, had and have a soul plan for the interactions between Earth and the Sun. This Cosmic Soul Plan insures that the sun and Earth will work in positive concert throughout the life of this galaxy; there are no mistakes, no miscalculations. It is time, if you so choose, to know and accept that your planet, your sun, solar system and galaxy are not destined to destroy themselves. They have a sacred destiny in service to *All There Is*. You are approaching this mission yourselves by mastering self, leading to your world service.

Soon you will be ready to know that **the sun's activities maintain and sustain within itself the conscious creation**

forces of Creation. This is a process of the balance of giving and receiving. As with your planet Earth, the sun holds within its core **a planetary Creative BEing that oversees all that occurs within its physical and spiritual reality.** There are many ancient names for this Creator BEing, and they all represent Creation, not destruction. As with all of Creation, it loves what it creates since it is created from Love.

All those sun activities, be they storms, winds or flares are a full expression of the Love force that created the sun and your planet through Love. These sun activities support and love any and all life with its influence. All sacred solar action is an essential aspect of its natural growth and expansion, never to be feared or misunderstood by others whose intention may be to control you with misinformation. Fear is the absence of Love, and when you enter fear you are not able to integrate the positive Love energy benefits of solar or any other activities.

We, the Cosmic Keepers of Creation, who were and are so involved with the creation of all Suns (including the one that will be your home), ask that you now embrace the healing Light of your sun as an essential aspect of life on planet Earth. Place your hands upon your heart and take a deep breath and embrace your sun's warmth as you now know you are One with *All There Is*. If it resonates, as you did in ancient times, greet the sun each morning as it rises and in the evening when it sets. Shut off your mental body as you meditate, hear, and see what messages your sun has for you. This type of environment will be your home someday. That is why we have brought some new truths to you about the sun at this time.

DIVINE DISCUSSIONS

For now, as a conscious, living sentient being, your sun has the potential to be all the energy you need on your planet without the control of others or burdensome expense. As humans becoming multi-dimensional beings you have the ability to connect with all other sentient conscious higher realm beings to gain whatever truth and wisdom you need to evolve into your Divine Destiny of *Eternal BEings Of Light* in service to *All There Is*. Ask and ye shall receive in a balance of giving and receiving. How many of you never ask by not seeing yourself good or worthy enough to know?

A LIFE DIVINELY DEFINED

For over three decades, I worked with many very talented and successful people in the advertising and commercial film industries. At the end of my working life, I thought I would morph into quiet. I began my advertising career in the heady Man Power/Madison Avenue/Mad Men days of advertising in the early 1970s, at the top of the ad game at Young & Rubicam, 285 Madison Avenue, New York City. Y&R had the most prestigious accounts, creativity, and billing. It was a great place to work if your family could afford to send you there; their low starting salaries reflected their competitive entry value. Beyond the three-martini lunches in the haze of cigarette smoke, I would define myself.

After a few restless years, in which I changed departments four times (media to sales promotion to account management to creative), Y&R and I finally realized the advertising agency life was not in my Divine Soul Plan. I enrolled in New York University's film school and jumped to the other side of the advertising business: commercial film production. The ad agencies became my clients. My soul plan now linked me with some of the most gifted commercial and feature film directors in the world—the likes of Ridley and Tony Scott and George Lucas.

The Scott brothers and I, along with many other film people, founded Fairbanks Films, and that company took over the commercial film production advertising world in short order. We produced for Apple Computer founder, Steve Jobs, the famous 1984 TV spot that launched personal cyber technology into the world. Today, this commercial is still considered the most successful TV spot ever created. Mr. Jobs, I know you are still proud, wherever you are, since you put your job on the line for this production. Then the George Lucas film people decided they wanted to get into the advertising game and came knocking. Why not? After the film industry, the advertising business is one of the most influential and lucrative forms of communication.

So over to Lucasfilm I went with all their inventive digital technology. It's fair to say their division of Industrial Light & Magic taught the advertising world digital wizardry, even though others jumped on quickly. It was great fun being the Director of Marketing of the commercial division, teaching the ad world how to bring any image to the screen (without killing anyone) if they had enough money and time. We changed commercial film forever, producing thousands of spots shown worldwide. Many of these short films became household icons.

During my three decades in advertising and commercial film production, I got to know the planet up close and personal. It was more than anyone could ask of a career! So I thought when it came time to leave it, I surely would be ready for a more peaceful and quiet lifestyle. Wrong! If you are in the film production business, you get to know California really well. At least I thought I did. The weather, locations, studios and crews made California an alternative on any production schedule. Only strikes or clients with low budgets would prevent you from shooting in California. Fairbanks Films was my finishing school in Southern California, and the Lucasfilm organization provided my Northern California training. George Lucas preferred Northern California to the south, not resonating with Hollywood values.

While commuting to Northern California from my New York City office for Industrial Light & Magic commercials, or Lucasfilm, I often took time to explore wonders the west has to offer. One of my most memorable trips was driving near the top of Mount Shasta, just south of the Oregon border. Mount Shasta is part of the Cascade Mountains, a dramatic volcanic mountain range that snakes its way north into Washington State. The size and grandeur of this mother of mountains was amazing; you could see it from a hundred miles away. We have nothing like it on the East Coast. And I thought enjoying its wondrous size and beauty was enough at the time. I would later learn otherwise. Ten years later, I would return, 'awakened' for another purpose entirely.

Some say, as we grow older and get closer to leaving this world, we may become more spiritually conscious, closer to God Power; women become more masculine and men more feminine or something like that. Well, anyway, after some medical mishaps and the "enough is enough" syndrome, I did leave the film and advertising businesses.

What else was I going to do, produce another commercial? The last spot we did was the biggest commercial ever created. It was for Ford Motor Company; ninety days of shooting all over the world, the largest advertising budget ever, and aired around the globe. This was my perfect swan song. Did I need another cue to exit? No! And there was this curious notion that something inside me was yearning to express a new sense of self. Something else was next, but I had no idea what it was. Surrendering to the unknown really challenged my mind, which always had to know.

My mother was of Native American descent and my father was Irish. My father's Celtic grandmother, my great-grandmother, was a backwoods Alabama healer. I call it my "I-and-I" links (Irish and Indian, both known for native healing). I remember sitting by my great grandmother's bedside as a young child, listening to her stories of her healing potions and how people would walk for days to get to her for a "healing." She knew how to pick herbs from the forest floor and to turn pine-tree sap into a soothing medicine. So I imagined this ability was also in my DNA. It was.

Filmmakers are often multifaceted people. Once, while working with one of my film directors on a project, I developed a cold and shared my family's healing background. My film director friend immediately suggested that I see his alternative medicine doctor, Dr. Herbert Fill. This particular director knew I was at the end of my film career, and there was more to cure than a cold. Dr. Fill was a rare mix of psychiatrist, acupuncturist and homeopath. He had been a commissioner of mental health for the City of New York, working from a Park Avenue office that he ran by himself. It was not long before the patient became a student of alternative medicine under Dr. Fill. This was my transition from advertising into the 'healing arts.'

Once my transition—or should I say, my transformation—began, it went fairly quickly. After a couple of years studying under Dr. Fill, I easily moved into training for Reiki (the energy therapy) and light ascension and became certified in these. These new alternative medical worlds introduced me to an entirely new community of people not associated with advertising or film. I began to know this was not going to be the beginning of a quiet retirement but a reinvention of myself through a broader use of all my talents and gifts.

The next transition took me into other higher-realm dimensions, not unlike the worlds George Lucas brought to the silver screen. Maybe that's the reason my career included the Lucas organization—to better prepare me for what was to come. Anyhow, what transpired next felt organic, extraordinary, and natural at the same time. And I realized many of George Lucas's stories were real.

The next destination/stop on my transformation train took me on a sacred journey to Egypt, where I connected with higher beings in the King's Chamber of the Great Pyramid. Later, I considered working with New York Times best-selling author Neale Donald Walsch of the *Conversations with God* books and began to connect with higher beings myself. If George Lucas could imagine other worlds that gave us hope and people like Neale Donald Walsh could communicate with God, why couldn't I do something similar?

As I was often enthralled by divine messengers (God, Archangels, Galaxy and Star Beings), could I listen to the message, apply it, and see if it could improve my life or the lives of others? Yes, I could! Today, millions of people worldwide connect with multiple dimensions through cyberspace, books, films, workshops or by directly experiencing messages from other realms. Can we accept wisdom from sources other than the human mind? That is the question of the day. The number of people connecting beyond the human mind seems to increase daily. Something is shifting, not only in me but also in the world. We are beginning to realize that we are not alone; our planet, our galaxy, and the universe are more diverse than we ever imagined, and there is a plan in it all. And we need the help of those other realms if we are to grow and evolve in a healthy way.

Through years of personal processing work and working with others who were already 'connecting,' I began to trust and know that ours was not the only frequency/dimension in existence (Einstein and string theory physicists had already suggested this). Now I would begin to connect with these higher frequencies myself along with many others. OK, I want to be the first to acknowledge this is the tricky part for some. I too come from a world that says, "If you cannot show me or prove it, it does not exist." Some people simply will not be able to accept or believe my story from this point on. For those who know the truth, that's cool, a gift. For those who cannot accept what is being said, or see it simply as fiction or untrue, that's okay. The mind believes; the heart knows. But try to apply the message, if it resonates.

A Sacred Ritual

Ten years after my first journey to Mount Shasta, I returned there as a transformed man with a lot of hardcore business experience behind me. I joined other like-minded/spirited people on a sacred journey back to Mount Shasta. Little did I know ten years earlier that it was considered one of the most powerful spiritual portals on Earth. We were there to serve as proxies for humanity, performing specific rituals on the mountain to assist the planet and all of us to move into higher levels of consciousness through a unique opportunity called ascension—a consciousness of being at one with *All That Is*.

On our journey, we would heal some wounded aspects within ourselves, which allowed us to connect with a higher-dimensional civilization inside the planet that coexists with us and intends for us to join together with it in the future. Where was George Lucas now?

Later, I would co-found a website, The Angel News Network, and a metaphysical school to teach and share what I had learned. I began connecting with other like-minded/spirited people, writing and connecting more with various higher realms. Each day, I sense I am always at the beginning of an ever-growing process of a sense of self and an expanding universe.

So when you get ready for a life change, watch out! You never know what destiny (your soul plan) may have in store for you. You just might end up talking to angels and all sorts of higher-realm beings that define who you are and why you are here!

Phillip Elton Collins is a teacher, healing arts therapist, conscious channel, former journalist, ad man, author/poet, and cofounder of the Angel News Network in Ft. Lauderdale, New York City, and Los Angeles, and Modern Day Mystery School. His books include *Coming Home To Lemuria: An Ascension Adventure Story* (being adapted into a stage play and screenplay), *Sacred Poetry & Mystical Messages: To Change Your Life & The World* (116 original poems and twenty Inner Earth messages), *Man Power God Power* (a volume of higher realm teachings), *The Happiness Handbook: Being Present Is The Present: Phrases of Presence To Set Us Free To Be...Happy, Activate Your Soul Plan: Angel Answers & Actions*, and *God's Glossary: A Divine Dictionary* (definitions directly received from whence we all came). These books divinely define this author.

www.ingramcontent.com/pod-product-compliance
Lightning Source LLC
Chambersburg PA
CBHW020923090426
42736CB00010B/1015